THE CRAFT OF
Chair Seat Weaving

with cane, rush, splint, and rope

George Sterns

Interweave Press

Illustrations by Ann Sabin
Cover design by Signorella Graphics
Cover and color photography (except where noted) by Joe Coca
Step-by-step photography by Barbara Liebler
Production by Marc McCoy Owens
Copyediting by Betsy Strauch

Interweave Press
201 East Fourth Street
Loveland, Colorado 80537
(303) 669-7672

Library of Congress Catalog Number 90-4591
ISBN 0-934026-56-4
First printing: 1990
10M:1190:CL:OB

Library of Congress Cataloging-in Publication Data
Sterns, George, 1922–
    The Craft of Chair Seat Weaving: with cane, rush, splint, and
rope / by George Sterns.
        p.   cm.
    Includes bibliographical references (p.
    Includes index.
    ISBN 0-934026-56-4 : $18.95
    I. Title
TT199.S78   1990
684.1'3--dc20   90-4591
                                                    CIP

Dedication

For the assistance, guidance, and support provided by two patient editors, Barbara Liebler and Jane Patrick, my sincere gratitude. To the generous individuals who consented to the Gallery and to my many clients over the years, my thanks. All of you have made this possible.

Acknowledgments

These people and firms have contributed in large and small ways to this book:

Virginia Zordani of Tole House Antiques; Robert Spindle and Kelso Lynn of Country Club Furniture Shop; Jim Moore of Penthouse (formerly Tru Grain); Dale and Sue Slaughter of D & S Enterprises; Kevin Cyr (and also, at one time, John Matchael) of The Woodshop, Carbondale, Colorado; Earl Fox and Jud Lively of Old Country Refinishing.

In many diverse ways the following have been a great help, too: Paul and Bertha Tschetter, Marian Miller, John Lovins. My parents, George and Lillie Sterns, are last but not least.

And those no longer with us bring delightful memories: Dr. Giles Filley and Marian Talmadge. Would that I might do the same.

If I should live to a ripe old age,

May I possess some bit of individuality, charm, and wit

That I may not be discarded when I am withered, worn, and weak,

But sought after and cherished like a fine antique.

—Anonymous

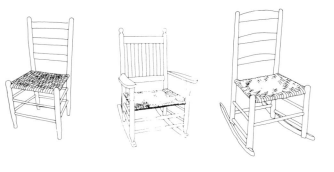

Contents

FOREWORD

We have come a long way from the days when only royalty was permitted to sit.

The throne signifies rank and privilege, reflected in the words "the chair", "chairman", and "to sit". Parliaments, legislatures, juries, and judges are said to "sit" when they convene, indicating deliberations of considerable importance. In the course of time, chairs have spread from the top to the bottom (literally) of our society. Chairs are now taken for granted as part of our earthly goods. A throne in our day is more likely to be a smooth number in white porcelain than it is an ornamental perch for someone of noble birth.

Chairs have evolved mostly in wood, with simple or elaborate methods for filling in the seat area. Seating materials and methods for making a seat attractive, comfortable, and durable cover a broad spectrum. Several of these materials and the craft of working them are addressed here. I hope these skills will bring you as much satisfaction as they have to me. I acquired them over many years of trial and error with chairs of all sizes and shapes. I can't help but think that the chairs that found their way to my workshop must have been just as colorful as the people who made them. Imagine the craftsmen who created some of these classics, all chair types which I've worked with at one time or another in my workshop: the rare American primitives with their severe lines primly upright; the genteel American versions of Chippendale and Hepplewhite, which must have graced many a candlelit dinner; the fancy Sheraton and Hitchcock styles with the glitter of gold and color that echoed the Empire style of Napoleon; the country rockers and slat-backs that witnessed many a bountiful harvest; the quiet, elegant refinement of the Shakers, whose sense of proportion may never be surpassed; the robust Victorians in sensuous curves and carvings; the "modern" Eastlake that abandoned curves and consumed walnut in vast amounts; the graceful, airy French styles of the eighteenth century in a setting of marble and gilt; the ultramodern products of 1920s Bauhaus, whose designs are still "modern" 60 years later; the Danish designs in teak by Hans Wegner with their smooth, unadorned, flowing lines; the simplicity of Swedish chairs, a rebirth of Shaker functionalism; the nondescript chair without provenance or pedigree that holds the memory of someone who lived and loved.

Each chair has its own personality; each has an unmistakable presence; each warmly invites your acquaintance. My work with chairs has been a voyage of discovery among styles and techniques. I sincerely wish you a safe and prosperous journey in your voyage of discovery.

INTRODUCTION

Necessity, more than anything else, triggered my interest in caning. At the depth of the Depression, about 1932 to 1934, when I was 10 to 12, my father took any job that he could get. He was a carpenter by trade, but in those days it was hard to find work in that line. So when a caning job came along, he tackled it with thankfulness and courage. He had no idea how it was done; he had no help or written directions. He learned by trial and error, and in the process I learned, too. When all the wrong ways and dead ends had been thoroughly explored, we blundered onto the right way, and the experience stuck like oatmeal to my ribs. The pay was pitiful, three or four cents a hole, for an average price on a cane seat that totaled about three dollars. And the time! In the beginning, it took three or four days to worry the job to completion.

We did cane seats infrequently; the income they produced was not enough to live on. Other work, if there was any, had to fill the large gaps in between.

My life improved slowly after that period. When World War II arrived, my career was interrupted for three and a half years as I became a radio operator on a rescue boat in Burma, working for the OSS. We hauled "agents" (spies) to remote spots on the Arakan coast. After that diversion, I returned home to finish college, majoring in fine arts. A glut of veterans emerged from schools across the land, and my livelihood gravitated into drafting of one kind or another. Eventually I headed a small unit of artists and manuscript typists in the publication department of a large company. When layoffs befell us, I laid off my empire, and then I resigned.

By then I had become acquainted with some local caners. Two of them passed away about the time I departed the corporate world, so there was a vacuum to fill. I began again as a caner. This occupational shift got off to a slow start, but I found there were certain advantages: no time clock, no commute, and no overlords and underlings. I was located in my own home and had a wonderful feeling of freedom. After a thin year, my clientele increased and began to keep me occupied.

Thus began a twenty-five-year stint in caning. The customers and chairs came to my shop in end-less variety. One year there were over seven hundred pieces. More normal years brought four to five hundred.

In 1976, a Denver newspaper did an article on my cane business, set up by one of my clients. The interview helped me recognize the positive aspects of caning: 99 percent of the customers were a delight to know and a pleasure to do business with. As my clientele grew from individuals to shops dealing in furniture repair and refinishing, upholstery, interior decorating, and office furniture, interesting requests came in: "Make a cane privacy screen to fit between the desk pedestals."

Should you choose caning as a hobby or a profession, your experiences will prove to be varied, interesting, and deeply satisfying. The large variety of chairs requiring seats will help chase boredom. I think you'll find that there's never a dull moment. The stories these chairs suggest, the mysteries they hint at, and the aura of a famous owner all add spice to the restoration of a piece. No, you may not find yourself awash in money, but you will have a wealth of a special kind, and that's what life's about. You have my wholehearted encouragement in your endeavors.

ABOUT THIS BOOK

This book is for caners of some experience who may have had problems that have gone unsolved for one reason or the other. This book is also for the beginner, who I hope will find enough information and guidance to work a job from start to finish.

Each chapter in this book stands pretty much alone, and in instances where additional information can be found in another part of the text, I've referred you to that section. Although you may find yourself turning to a chapter for the specific job at hand, I encourage you to survey the various techniques for their similarities and differences. As a beginning, I've given a brief overview of the different techniques covered herein.

The four large divisions covered in this book are cane, both hand cane and machine cane; rush, including imitation and natural; wide cane and its near relative, splint; and Danish rope. These fairly well cover the caner's world. There are miscellaneous patterns here and there, but they can be tossed into one or the other of these large bins. Though you may find yourself drawn to one specialty of the four categories, your best bet is to get a broad experience in all of them. They enhance each other.

Anatomy of a Chair

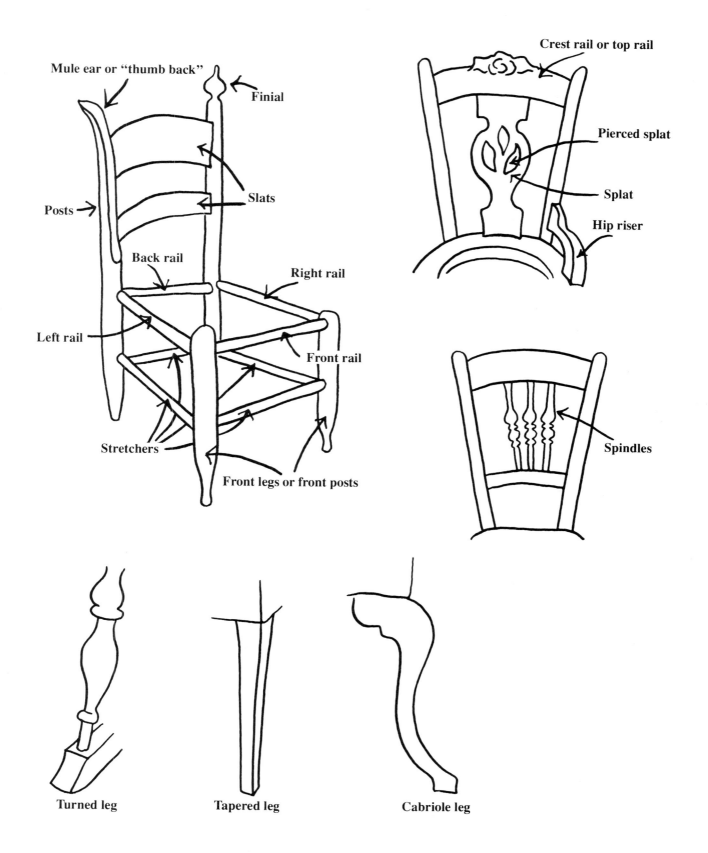

Mule ear or "thumb back"

Finial

Posts

Slats

Back rail

Right rail

Left rail

Front rail

Stretchers

Front legs or front posts

Crest rail or top rail

Pierced splat

Splat

Hip riser

Spindles

Turned leg

Tapered leg

Cabriole leg

HAND CANING

CHAPTER 1

An American, factory-made chair from about 1870 to 1890 with a hand-caned seat. A huge number of this type, in an endless variety, survive to this day. They are sturdy, functional, and comfortable. Courtesy of Erich Callmann.

A practice frame
Horseshoes or balloons
Other shapes
  round or elliptical
  convex
  concave
Special techniques
  French caning
  pegged cane
  double cane, not pegged
  suspended medallion
  bentwood
Plastic cane
Finishing hand cane
Patching hand cane

❖ The word "wicker" can loosely be described as a basketry technique applied to furniture construction. The materials in wickerwork may include rattan, though willow, reed, or other materials are sometimes used. Wickerwork is quite a different technique from that of woven chair seats, and is not discussed in this book.

Although the word "cane" can refer to a long stick or a field in which sugar is raised, the cane used in chair seat weaving is a long, very tough, shiny strand cut from the inner bark of the rattan palm (*Calamus* sp. and *Daemonorops* sp.). This climbing palm grows in the jungles of Southeast Asia, including Sumatra and Malaysia; most cane is processed in Singapore and Hong Kong. Reed is obtained from the pithy core of the rattan palm, is cut into narrow shapes, round, flat, and wedge-shaped (spline)—and sizes in relatively long lengths. Reed is also used in chair seat weaving.

Chairs that are prospects for hand caning all have one thing in common: a row of holes around the edge of the seat or back frame. Frame shapes are many: square, horseshoe, round, trapezoidal, concave, or convex. Not surprisingly, a square frame is the simplest one of these to cane; the others are the offspring of this Adam, so to speak. Since complications multiply rapidly as the shape to be caned becomes more complex, I suggest that you learn the rudiments of caning by weaving a square practice frame. With this exercise completed, you will move confidently to the next more complicated job, the balloon or

horseshoe, without trauma or hysteria. One small, easy step at a time is the way to go, and the first one is an introduction to the material and a word on the few tools you will need.

TOOLS AND MATERIALS

Select cane of the appropriate size so that your work is not more difficult than it needs to be. Matching the material of the existing chair seat is probably a good guide, though be aware that the seat you are replacing may have been an amateurish job. If there is no existing seat to use as a guide, you'll need to determine the correct cane size by measuring the size of the holes and the distance from hole center to hole center. Consult and follow the table of cane and hole spacing in Appendix B. You can depart from the listed sizes, but not very far. Choosing cane that is too small for the hole spacing will result in an open, weak, short-lived seat. It's a piece of cake to weave but it won't last a month. Choosing cane that is too large causes multiple trauma to the caner and to the cane: broken cane, shredded cane, jammed holes, and a fuming caner.

Chair cane comes in 1000-foot hanks consisting of 6- to 20-foot lengths. Specify Long Select First Quality when ordering; nothing less will do. One hank does about four average-sized seats, or buy a 250-foot bunch for one seat. To help make the hank more manageable, dip it briefly in water and hang it up to straighten. Do *not* untie the string at the top of the loops. If it breaks, tie on another, or the cane will become hopelessly tangled.

You can purchase cane from a specialty craft or caning store. If you cannot find a local retail outlet, you can order by mail from one of the suppliers listed at the back of the book.

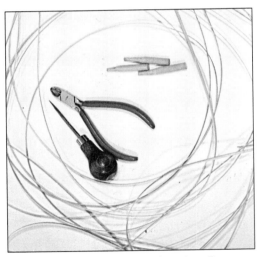

Tools and materials for hand caning: Long Select First Quality hand cane in the appropriate size to weave the web, binding and lacing cane for the border, 4- to 5-inch side-cutting pliers, a 4-inch pick or awl, and wooden pegs.

A few simple tools are required for seat weaving. The most important is the human hand, with brain attached. Actually, two hands are needed; if you are not ambidextrous already, you soon will be. You'll need a pair of 4- to 5-inch side-cutting pliers and a 4-inch pick or awl. The best awl is one used for leather work, with a thin shaft and a wooden handle. A carpenter's awl or an ice pick is too long. Even though there is such a thing as a "caning needle", I find it a useless curiosity.

You will need wooden pegs, and homemade ones will serve better than any others. Cut a ³/₁₆-inch-diameter birch dowel into 1- to 1¼-inch lengths. Holding one of these lengths vertically on a soft pine block, use a very sharp knife to shave it carefully into a long taper, rotating the peg as you slice. The point should be about ¹/₈-inch in diameter. Make a few dozen pegs for ordinary caning jobs. These will do for the majority of cane seats. For seats with slightly larger holes, make pegs from ¹/₄-inch dowel stock. Alternatively, you can cut and taper dry hardwood twigs of the appropriate size.

Store-bought pegs have limited use. The tops are too fat and stick up too far. They are impossible for pegged French cane which has many very small holes. Golf tees have the wrong taper, and the painted finish makes them too slippery to stay stuck. Large nails have no taper and slide right out. Pencil stubs sharpened in a pencil sharpener, or dowels sharpened the same way, have too steep a taper and will not hold. Round rattan can be used in a pinch, but the point will break off. These substitutes have all been tried and found wanting. Go with birch dowels and avoid anguish.

PREPARATION

Soak the cane in a small dishpan or squat bucket of water for 10 to 30 minutes to soften it for working. Some caners add glycerine to the water to make the cane hold dampness longer, or Ivory soap to make the cane slide through the web more easily, but both are totally unnecessary. Gently shake the hank as you pull out one strand at a time. Pull out and coil up four strands and plunk them in the dishpan or bucket. As cane is used, add several more lengths to the water so that you have a wet supply.

Cane can be left in water overnight without harm, but if left two or three days, it will begin to grow things and get scummy. Replace the water every day.

Cane has a right and wrong side. The shiny side is the public side, always kept facing you; the dull side is the back (figure 1.1).

To weave with the cane, take one strand from the water and determine the "weaving end" and the "tie end". The strand has a node or bump about every foot (figure 1.2). Usually each node has been shaved slightly. If you run your finger back and forth across a node, you'll notice that it feels smooth in one direction and rough in the other direction. The rough side of the node is the growing end of the vine, the tying end of a length of cane. The smooth side of the node points toward the root end of the plant and is always the weaving end. Examine several bumps to be sure that you've got the ends identified correctly. This determination is critical; when you use the correct end for weaving, the nodes slide easily without catching or tearing. This saves a great deal of grief.

1.1 The shiny, slightly rounded side of the cane should face up on the top of the seat and down on the underside.

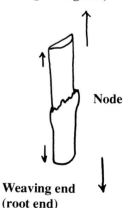

1.2 Examine one or more nodes to determine the weaving end of the cane.

HAND CANING A PRACTICE FRAME

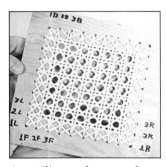

A rectilinear shape, such as this square practice frame, makes a good beginning caning project.

❖ Most books set forth the Seven-Step Method as the technique to use for hand caning. This is not the method I use here because I find that steps one through four of the Seven-Step Method present difficulties in the layout of certain non-rectilinear shapes. In addition, I find that cane applied by the Seven-Step Method has a tendency to become overly taut, to the detriment of the wood frame and the cane itself.

Because the traditional cane pattern is based on a square, the simplest frame to weave it on is a square one. (A rectangle that is only slightly wider than it is high is also acceptable for this first venture.) This exercise will introduce you to the steps in making the cane pattern and will give you practice in handling the cane itself. If you are a beginner, you will profit greatly by weaving a practice board before trying the balloon shape. If you have some experience, you will do well to review this section on the square because we will use this method in the caning to follow. My method may differ somewhat from the technique you have been using.

In real-life caning, the square or rectangular frame may never present itself on a chair seat, though you might find one on a stool. If you don't have a rectilinear stool, make a square of ³/₄-inch-thick plywood. Figure 1.3 gives the dimensions and shows where to drill the holes. The size of this board need not be exactly as shown, but too small is like engraving on the head of a pin, and too large means *beaucoup* weaving, which is no great sin: the exercise will do you good. Sand or file the edges and corners of the board to minimize splinters. Label the holes with numbers running left to right on the front and back

frame pieces, and front to back on the two sides. To make the instructions easier to follow, label each front hole with an F, each back hole with a B, each left hole with an L, and each right hole with an R. Or just keep these numbers and letters in your head as you would with a real chair seat.

Choose Medium (3 mm) cane for this hole size and spacing.

Weaving a chair seat progresses by steps. First, pairs of verticals are installed front to back, then pairs of horizontals are woven, then two sets of diagonals (one from back left to front right; and another from front left to back right) are laced through to complete the weaving. Finally, a border or binding is worked around the edges to cover the holes and to give the seat a tidy finish.

Weaving the Verticals

To begin the first pair of verticals, find the tie end of a wet piece of cane. It's a time saver to weave the first three holes with this end, even though the cane slides more easily through the holes in the other direction. With the tie end, go down hole 3B, come up in hole 2B (figure 1.4). Bring the cane to the front hole at 2F. Leave 4 inches of cane hang-

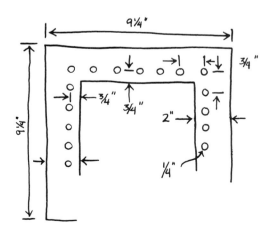

1.3 A square practice frame of ³/₄-inch plywood.

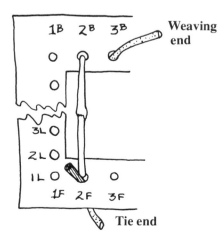

1.4 Begin the verticals at hole 3B. Weave the tie end as shown. Leave a 4-inch tail hanging below the front of the frame and temporarily peg it at hole 2F.

ing down below the front frame at hole 2F. This will be tied later. Temporarily peg the cane at hole 2F.

To ensure that the cane is shiny side out as you weave, always back the cane through your fingers until you reach the weaving end. Do not allow it to twist or flop over. Turn the cane within each hole so that the shiny side is toward the floor as the cane goes from one hole to the next on the underside of the frame, then turn it again as it comes up through the next hole so that it is shiny side up on the top of the seat, as shown in figure 1.1.

Keep only enough tension so that the cane lies straight and flat. Pull firmly but do not try to pull the strand tight like a guitar string. There should be a slight give when you place a finger on the center of a woven cane.

Now that you have woven backward and secured the tie end, it is time to continue with the weaving end. Bring it to the front and down hole 3F, then across to hole 2F (figure 1.5). Pull the cane through these two holes by holding a finger in the bottom loop of cane on the underside of the frame and allowing the cane to run loosely over the finger. This helps the cane to run freely from hole to hole without binding. When all the cane has been pulled through, tighten the cane from hole 3F

to hole 2F on the underside, checking (usually by touch) that the shiny side points to the floor. Bring the cane to the back, go down hole 2B and come up in hole 3B (figure 1.6). Pull the cane through. Bring the weaver to hole 3F, go down this hole, and come up in hole 4F (figure 1.7). Now you have com-

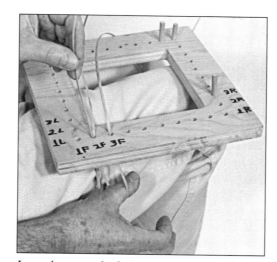

Lace the cane clockwise around holes 2 and 3 front and back until there are two canes at each location, then move to the right and repeat the two-hole clockwise rotation.

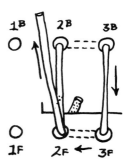

1.5 Bring the weaving end to the front and down hole 3F, then up in hole 2F.

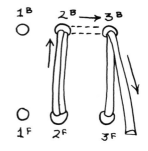

1.6 Go down hole 2B and come up in hole 3B.

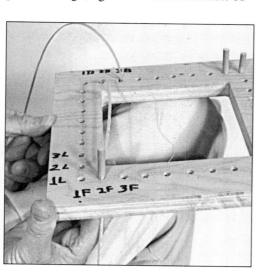

Weave the verticals first.

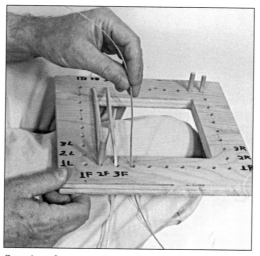

Starting the second pass: bring the weaving end to the front and down hole 3F, then up in hole 4F. Hold a finger in the bottom loop of the cane below the frame as you pull the cane through these two holes.

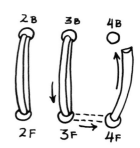

1.7 To complete the first set of vertical pairs, bring the weaver to hole 3F, go down this hole, and come up in hole 4F.

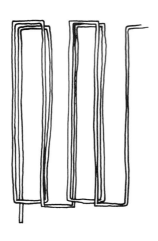

1.8 Repeat this pattern across the seat: make two clockwise circles of cane between a pair of front and a pair of back holes, then move one hole to the right on the front rail and again make two clockwise circles between pairs of holes.

pleted the first set of vertical pairs and have set the stage for lacing the next pair of verticals. The cane has gone clockwise around holes 2 and 3 front and back until there are two canes at each location; then it moves to the right one hole to begin the next clockwise rotation for two pairs. Continue to make pairs of verticals in this way across to the right side

of the frame, repeating the pattern of figure 1.7 as shown in the diagram of figure 1.8. Check that you have a pair of verticals in every hole except the corner holes, one cane sitting on top of the other. Peg the last vertical where it goes down the last hole in the front of the frame before the 1R corner hole (figure 1.9).

Weaving the Horizontals

If your weaving end is short, peg it and start weaving the horizontals with a new, damp cane, weaving the first three holes backward with the tie end of the cane as you did when you wove the verticals (figure 1.10). Weave this tie end across, going *between* the top vertical and the bottom vertical of each pair. Take the tie end down hole 2L with at least 4 inches extra to tie and peg it to hold it temporarily. One horizontal of the first pair is now woven, and the weaving end will be ready to weave from the right. But it must wait for now until you are ready to continue.

Like verticals, the horizontals are worked in pairs. But while we put in the pairs of verticals with one continuous cane, you can make the horizontal pairs by working with two different canes going in opposite directions. This will evenly distribute the loops of the horizontal canes on the underside. Allow the

weaving end of the first horizontal cane to rest while you start its partner. With a new, damp cane, take the tie end down hole 3L and come up in hole 2L (figure 1.11). Weave across, going *over* the top vertical and *under* the bottom vertical of each pair, by moving the top vertical slightly to the left. Take the tie end down hole 2R and peg it, leaving a 4-inch tail below the frame.

The first pair of horizontals is now in place, and the seat is set up with two canes ready to weave in opposite directions. From the left, weave *under* where you wove *over* in the last row, and over where you wove under, and so on (figure 1.12). After weaving across, pull the cane just enough that it lies flat. Straighten the row with your fingernails. Let this long cane hang on the right side toward the front of the frame, out of the way (figure 1.13). Now take the cane coming out of 3R

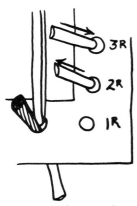

1.9 Peg the last vertical where it goes down the last hole before the corner hole in the front of the frame.

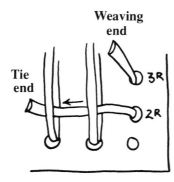

1.10 Start the horizontals the same way you did the verticals by weaving the first three holes backward with the tie end of the cane.

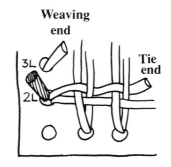

1.11 With a new piece of cane, weave across, going over the top vertical and under the bottom vertical of each pair.

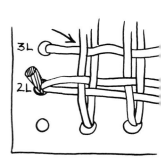

1.12 With the weaving end of cane on the left, weave opposite to the previous row.

and weave it across, weaving the opposite over-under pattern to the row just completed. Pull the strand through the weaving and straighten it. Weave down through hole 3L and come up in hole 4L. This completes the second pair of horizontals. Repeat for the rest of the horizontals. When you reach the back, you'll find that there won't be much space for your fingers to work the last horizontal row. Use the awl to lift the verticals so that you can easily slip the cane underneath.

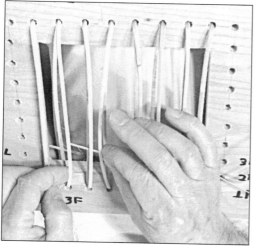

When you have completed the verticals, if the cane is long enough, it can be used to weave the first horizontal. If you need to add a new length of cane, follow the procedure for beginning a cane as shown in figure 1.10.

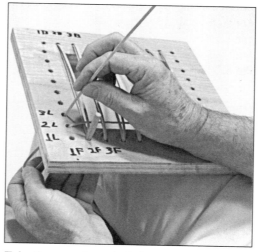

Take the cane down hole 2L and up in hole 3L. Leave this weaving end hanging free from hole 3L.

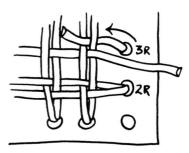

1.13 Let the strand from the last row hang out of the way while you weave across to the other side with the second strand.

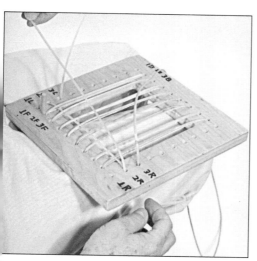

Begin a new horizontal cane from the right to make an opposing pair. Weave backward from hole 3R with the tie end as you've done before.

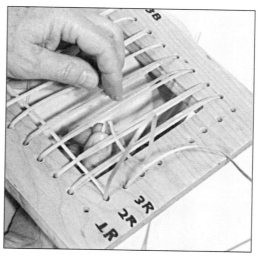

As you weave the second horizontal of any pair, move the upper vertical to the left. It helps to put a crimp in the end of the cane, as shown here.

❖ The first horizontal always goes between the top and bottom verticals.

❖ Add cane as needed, weaving backward for three holes as you did in the beginning.

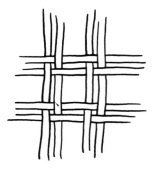

1.14 The vertical and horizontal pairs should be even and the "windows" easily visible.

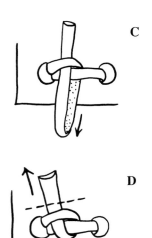

1.15 Tying off the ends on the underside of the seat.

Straighten the vertical and horizontal pairs so that they are reasonably even and the "windows" are easily visible (figure 1.14). If you drag wet fingers across the woven canes, they will stay in place when straightened with your fingernails.

Before you begin to weave the diagonals, tie off the ends on the underside to get them out of the way. Turn the board over. Poke the cane under one of the loops on the underside with the short end of the cane going toward the outside edge of the frame (figure 1.15A). Use the awl to lift the loop slightly to make

room. Keep the smooth side of this tail against the frame, leaving about a 1-inch loop. Turn the cane back toward the inside of the frame (figure 1.15B), inserting it through the loop. Pull the first loop tight (figure 1.15C), then pull the cane end tight (figure 1.15D). Cut off the end with side-cutting pliers about $1/8$-inch from the knot.

As you tie, distribute the knots around the perimeter of the frame, not allowing them to bunch up at one hole. Remove the pegs after tying off if they haven't fallen out by themselves.

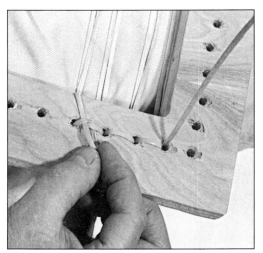

When a length of cane runs out, knot it on the back and begin a new cane (see figure 1.15).

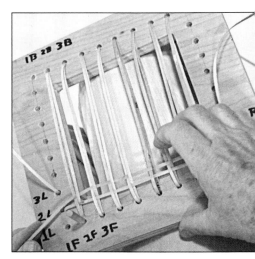

Use your fingernails to pull the horizontal cane into line.

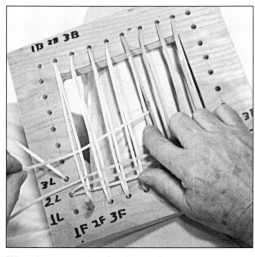

Weaving opposing horizontals.

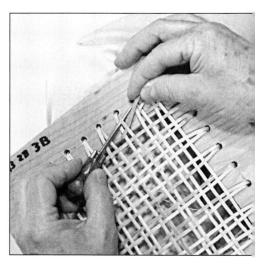

When weaving the last horizontal, you may need the awl to make room for the end.

Weaving the Diagonals

The diagonals are woven through the "windows" formed by openings in the pairs of horizontals and verticals. There are two sets of diagonals: one which weaves from the back left to the right front, and another set which weaves at right angles to the first, from the front left to the back right.

We'll start with the diagonals from the back left to the right front. If there was a long length left over from weaving the horizontals, you can begin weaving the diagonals with this end as is done here. Otherwise, you'll need to start with a new, wet cane and begin with the tie end as you've done before.

Begin weaving from the corner hole. Weave diagonally across the web going *under* each vertical pair and *over* each horizontal pair (figure 1.16). Go through the window each time, never between two strands of the same pair. When you reach the other side, go down the corner hole and up into the next hole (in either direction—it doesn't matter here) and weave back toward the other side. As you did with the first diagonal, weave *under* all the verticals and *over* all the horizontals. When you reach the other side, go down the corresponding hole and up into the corner hole again. You'll now have two diagonal strands coming out of this corner hole. When diagonal strands go through the same hole, the shape created by them is called a "fishhead". You'll have four of these in this practice frame, one at each corner. While fishheads are a rarity in this straight-edged practice frame, you'll discover later that they occur frequently in more complex shapes where fishheads are used to help fit a rectilinear interlacement into a nonrectilinear shape.

Achieving a uniform and correct interlacement around the edge of your chair seat is one of the skills which distinguishes an expert caning job from an amateurish one. Determining how the strands go into the holes and which ones is the key to an expert job. With our practice frame, there are not many decisions to make about which holes to go into—the more complex the shape, the more decisions there are to make. Use this practice frame to start training your eye to see the in-

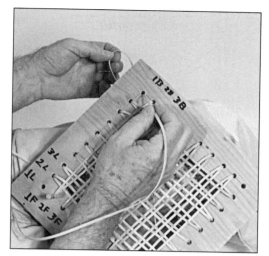

Begin the diagonals from back left to front right. Weave under *every vertical and* over *every horizontal pair.*

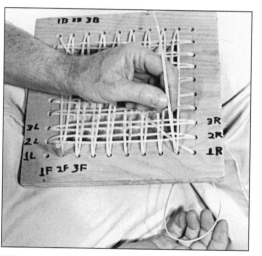

When you reach the opposite corner, go down hole 1R and come up in the next hole in either direction.

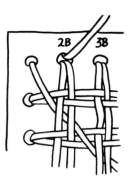

1.16 For all diagonals that weave from the back left to the front right, take the weaver *under* each vertical pair and *over* each horizontal pair. Go through the window each time, never between two strands of the same pair.

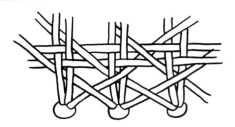

1.17 The four sides of our practice frame will have "Xs": a diagonal crosses a pair of canes coming from the adjacent hole before it begins its journey across the seat.

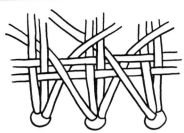

1.18 If a horizontal or vertical pair is missed at the edge, "Vs", a no-no in caning, are formed.

correct

Slides

incorrect

Binds

1.19 A correctly woven diagonal will slip easily into the overlap at the corner of each window. An incorrect diagonal will bind at the window corner, making it difficult to pull the strand through.

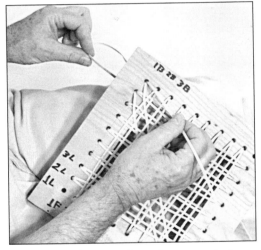

Two diagonals woven from the corner hole form a fishhead.

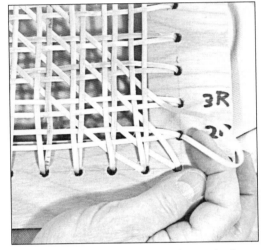

Note that the cane goes under the vertical pair and over the horizontal pair at the fishhead just as it does elsewhere.

terlacements your strands make along the edges of the caning. Think of the pattern at the edges created by the crossing of the strands as "Xs"(figure 1.17). With this pattern firmly in mind, use this to determine whether you need to weave over a vertical or horizontal set of strands at the edge. In other words, don't stop weaving too soon at the edge, a common mistake among beginners and, I'm afraid, many professional caners alike. You'll know if you've woven incorrectly if the pattern at the edge forms a "V"instead of an "X" (figures 1.17 and 1.18).

A correctly woven diagonal will slip easily into the overlap at the corner of each window. An incorrect diagonal will bind at each corner (figure 1.19) and will be difficult to pull

through. Whole seats have been woven with wrong diagonals, but they took a month of Sundays to do and resulted in shredded and broken cane, as well as a frustrated caner.

As you begin each wet cane, you will be able to take two or three "stitches" before pulling the rest of the length through. It will squeak from the surplus water. After the cane has dried a little, you can take three or four stitches at a time. Keep the working end of the cane short, only 2 or 3 inches long, and keep the smooth side of the cane up at all times. As you pull the whole length of cane through with one hand, use the other hand to guide the rest of the cane length into the window so that it stays right side up. If it does flop over, back it out and start again.

As you take the weaver from one hole to the next, do not allow the loops on the underside to stack up. Too many loops overlapping on the underside will give a messy appearance to the bottom of the seat. Planning your path will help keep the underside loops evenly distributed. It is permissible to skip one hole on the underside if needed to improve the layout, but never skip more than one. Your touch on the underside will tell you what is happening there. Complete this set of diagonals (from back left to front right) and check for mistakes.

Next, insert the second set of diagonals at right angles to the first set of diagonals, beginning at hole 1L/1F (see figure 1.20). Weave from front left to back right, always weaving *over* each vertical pair and *under* each horizontal pair (opposite to the path of the other set of diagonals). Be sure that these diagonals slip into the overlap at the corner of each window and pull through easily. Once again, pre-plan the path of the weaver so that the loops on the underside are evenly distributed.

When the last set of diagonals is completed, tie off all of the tails on the underside (figure 1.15). If you are weaving an actual chair seat instead of a practice frame, you now need to weave a border, called the binding, around the edge of the weaving to finish the job. Working the border is shown in figure 1.41.

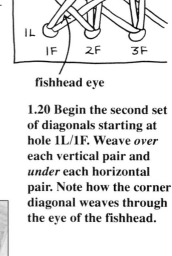

fishhead eye

1.20 Begin the second set of diagonals starting at hole 1L/1F. Weave *over* each vertical pair and *under* each horizontal pair. Note how the corner diagonal weaves through the eye of the fishhead.

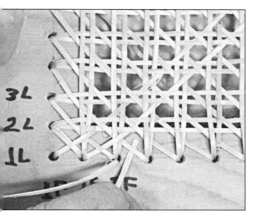

Beginning the second set of diagonals. Go under the horizontal pairs and over the verticals.

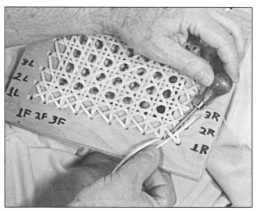

Weave through the "eye" of the fishhead at the corner (see figure 1.20).

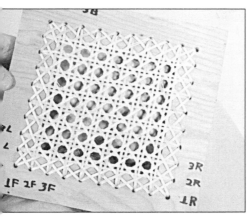

Your completed practice frame should look like this.

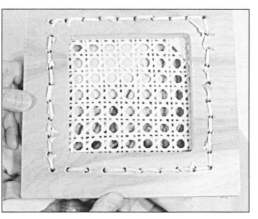

Knot all the ends neatly on the back.

❖ If the cane becomes dry while you are working, dampen it with a wet cloth.

HAND CANING A BALLOON OR HORSESHOE SEAT

A balloon-shaped seat can have a slightly curved rail like this chair or a straight back rail. A close relative is a horseshoe seat.

An irregular frame shape is the norm in caning; a perfect square or rectangle is rarely encountered. Now that you have practiced on a rectangle, you know the basic procedure for weaving the verticals, horizontals, and diagonals. On a seat with some curve in the side rail, you'll have layout decisions to make, and fishheads will occur in places other than the four corners.

Horseshoe-shaped seats and balloon seats are characteristic of American side chairs from about 1880 to 1900. They also appear on chairs in the Louis XVI style. Either a balloon or horseshoe shape would make a good first-time caning project.

Weaving the sides on the practice frame was straightforward with few complications. You didn't have to deal with curves, as you'll do here. In essence, the technique for straight sides and curved ones is the same, but the method of working them differs somewhat. On a rectilinear shape you could start the verticals at one side and work across to the other; with a horseshoe shape, you'll need to start the verticals in the center and work to either side. By starting in the center, you will automatically center the pattern on this kind of seat. This also lets you work from the easy part of the seat to the more difficult layout problems at the sides.

Begin by cutting away the old cane with a $3/4$-inch chisel. It is best to cut with a slicing motion, *away* from you and aimed slightly towards the center of the seat. Avoid damaging the wood, and cut the old cane even with the top face of the seat frame, slicing the cane off as it emerges from the holes. Turn the chair over and remove the cane loops on the bottom by sliding one corner of the chisel under the middle of the loop and prying up. If glue or paint has sealed the cane in the holes, they will have to be drilled out from the top of the seat, using an electric drill fitted with a twist drill of the same or slightly smaller diameter as the hole.

24

Weaving the Verticals

To find the center on the back rail, count the holes from the left corner to the right corner. Mark the center hole with tape or a peg. Count the holes in the front rail beginning at the join of the front and side rails (figure 1.21). If there are two center holes, peg both, front and back. If there are two centers on the back rail and only one on the front, you'll have to fudge, choosing one of the rear holes to pair with the front. The layout will be slightly skewed, but only an expert will notice.

Begin the verticals as you did on the practice frame by weaving backward with the tie end for three holes. Put the tie end down the rear center hole and come up in the next hole to the right (figure 1.22). Bring the tie end to the front, take it down the first hole to the right of center. Leave at least 4 inches to tie. You are now ready to continue with the weaving end, installing pairs of verticals (figures 1.23–1.25). Make verticals with this weaver, moving to the left until it runs out, then peg it. Come back to the right half of the seat and

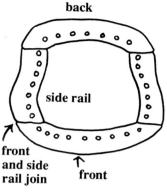

1.21 A balloon-shaped seat.

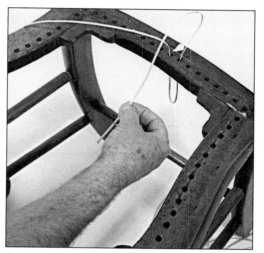

Soak the cane for 10 to 30 minutes. Bring the tie end up the hole right of the center back hole.

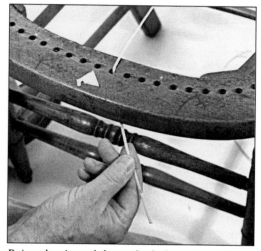

Bring the tie end down the hole to the right of center front. Leave 4 inches of cane below the frame to tie later.

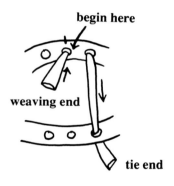

1.22 Begin the verticals by putting the tie end down the rear center hole and come up in the hole to the right. Peg the tie end in the front hole, the one to the right of center.

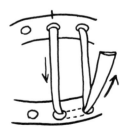

1.23 Bring the weaving end to the center front hole and up the next hole on the right.

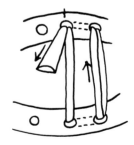

1.24 Continue with the weaver to the back and come up the center hole.

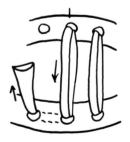

1.25 Take the weaver down the front center hole and move left one hole to start the pattern again.

❖ About 250 linear feet of cane are needed for an average-size chair seat.

❖ Contrary to popular thought, hand cane does not need to be pulled very taut. This activity wears out the caner and is hard on the cane and chair frame as well. Pull firmly, but don't exert a lot of tension. The cane should have some give.

❖ Since hand caning is a time-intensive endeavor, it is important to get as comfortable as possible. I like to sit on a low stool with the chair on the floor facing me.

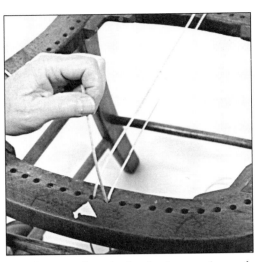

For the second vertical, take the weaving end of the cane down the center front hole and up in the next hole to the right.

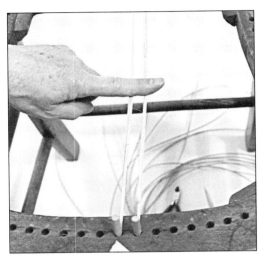

Check the tension in the middle with your finger.

start verticals next to the first pair of verticals and work to the right. This time you will be starting exactly as the verticals began on the practice square board (page 16). Pulling the cane through two holes in one movement saves much time. Repeat the pattern until you reach the right back corner hole. Check your work to see that each hole has a pair of canes in it.

There is now a lopsided semicircular opening at the right side of the seat. We must put some verticals into holes of the side rails to fill the semicircle, since the holes in the back rail are all used up. Which holes do we use?

To help you decide which holes will need verticals, imagine parallel lines spaced exactly as the verticals are spaced in the center of the seat superimposed on top of the chair seat in the as-yet-unwoven hole. If you need help in visualizing this, draw these lines on a piece of paper, and lay this lined paper over the empty semicircle, so that one or more of the lines are on top of existing verticals and the others are over the empty semicircle (figure 1.26). Note which holes in the side rail are closest to those lines and mark each with a peg. There will be some empty, unpegged holes where no line crosses. If a line passes, for example, *between* two holes at the back but *through* a hole at the front, you'll split the

vertical (called a half-split), as shown in figure 1.27. Two strands of a pair will come out of the front hole and will be split between the two holes at the back. If the line goes between two holes at both the back and the front, each strand of the vertical pair will go between separate holes (figure 1.28). In both cases these split verticals will act as a pair. Remember, there is never a single strand in either the verticals or the horizontals of a hand-caned pattern. As you gain experience in placing the verticals and horizontals in non-rectilinear seats, you can dispense with the lined paper; your eye will know.

When you've filled in the holes on the right side, peg the loose ends. If long enough, surplus cane can be used later for horizontals.

Return to the center and work vertical pairs to the left. On this half of the seat, the cane travels *counterclockwise* between two holes until there are two strands in each hole, then moves left under the front rail to the next hole.

When you reach the semicircle at the left, copy the vertical placement from the right. The two sides should match exactly (figure 1.27). Be sure the left strand of any half-split pair is on top of the right strand where they enter the front hole.

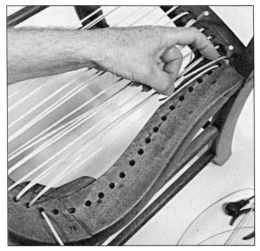

Continue installing the vertical pairs until you reach the hole to the left of the back corner hole. Peg the cane temporarily.

To maintain an even spacing of the verticals, you'll need to split some of them. Here, the vertical pair at the right front is divided between two holes at the back (a half-split vertical).

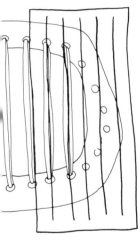

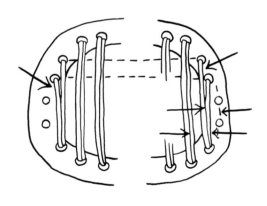

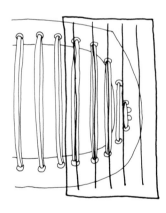

1.26 To determine where the verticals should go in the semicircular space along the curved side rail, superimpose parallel lines, spaced exactly as the verticals are spaced in the center of the seat. Lay this over the semicircle so that one or more of the lines are on top of the existing verticals and the others over the empty semicircle.

1.27 Half-split verticals. Two strands from one common hole at the front are divided between two holes at the back. The left cane should be on top of the right cane.

1.28 A fully-split vertical is necessary if the parallel line falls between two holes at both the front and the back. Each strand of a pair goes into a separate hole at the front and back. Remember, though, that these will be woven as a pair.

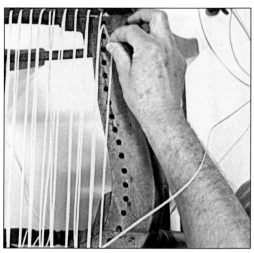

The next divided pair should be parallel to the other verticals and at the same spacing. Hold a length of cane in the correct position to judge which holes to use.

Putting in the last pair of verticals.

Return to the center of the seat and install the verticals counterclockwise from the center to the left.

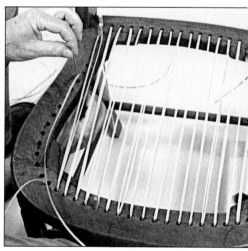

Complete the split canes on the left to match the split canes on the right. Whenever there are two verticals in the same hole, the left one must be on top.

Weaving the Horizontals

Now to the horizontals. Lay your lined paper horizontally on the seat with a line lying on the center front hole (figure 1.29). With pegs, mark the holes nearest the next line. The first horizontal pair of canes will go between these holes. If the line falls between two holes on each side, a split pair is called for. In this case, mark both holes on each side.

Proper spacing will produce Xs; starting the weaving too far back from the edge will make a strange-looking gap in the cane pattern; weaving too close to the front will produce Vs where there should be Xs (figure 1.30).

Start at the left hole (the one closer to the front if you have pegged two holes at each side), and weave the tie end across, between the top and bottom cane of each vertical pair, to the pegged hole on the right (figure 1.31). Weaving will be easier if you weave an inch or more back from the frame and pull the lower cane of each vertical pair down slightly to put the tie end through. Once across, poke the tie end down the hole, leaving a 4-inch tail, and peg to hold it until you come back later to tie it. Straighten the row.

If you have two pegged holes at each side for this first horizontal row, you'll need to make a split pair, which is usually the case with seats of this shape.

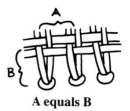

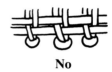

A equals B

No

1.30 The proper spacing.

Judge the position of the front horizontal cane by holding a piece across the chair (use a paper overlay as in figure 1.26 as necessary).

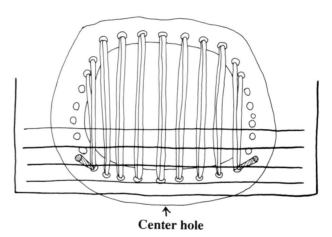

Center hole

1.29 Using horizontal parallel lines to determine where to start the horizontals. Place a line over the center hole, mark the holes nearest the next line at the sides of the front. The first horizontal pair of canes will be woven between these pegged holes. If the line falls between two holes on each side, split the pair.

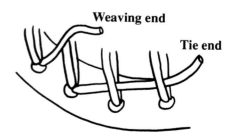

Weaving end

Tie end

1.31 Weave the first horizontal between the top and bottom cane of each vertical pair with a fresh, new cane. Straighten the row.

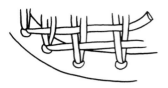

1.32 The second horizontal. With the weaving end, go over the top vertical strand of each pair.

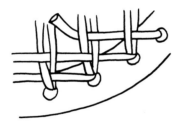

1.33 Bring the weaving end up in the next hole and weave the first strand of the second horizontal pair.

1.34 A split horizontal will accommodate the curve of the back rail.

For the second pass, weave across with the weaving end, going *under* the bottom verticals (figure 1.32). Remember, the top vertical always moves left. When you reach the pegged hole at the right, go down this hole and come up in the next one behind. Straighten the second horizontal with your fingernails and check for mistakes. Where the first horizontal goes under, the second horizontal goes over.

You have completed the first horizontal pair. If you are in doubt as to which holes the second pair of horizontals will go into, lay down your lined paper again to choose holes the correct distance back from the first horizontal row. Bring the weaving end up in the correct hole and weave across the first strand of the second horizontal pair (figure 1.33).

Take the weaver down the appropriate hole at the left and come up in the next hole back. Let this cane rest while you start the opposing cane, as you did with the rectangular practice frame. At the right rail, put the tie end of a fresh cane down one hole back of this last horizontal and come up in the same hole as its mate. This tie end completes the pair. The weaving end of the cane will rest for now and will be ready to continue later.

Weave the tie end across going in the opposite path to the first one. Note that the horizontal pair has a common hole on the left and a common hole on the right. When you reach the left rail, put this tie end down the same hole as the first cane of this pair, leaving 4 inches extra to tie, and peg to hold it until you come back later to tie.

Now the strand on the left and the strand on the right are ready to weave in opposite directions to make the next horizontal pair, just as you did for the square practice frame.

On reaching the back of the seat, another divided pair will accommodate the curve of the back rail. If you are not sure which holes to use, lay your lined paper down again, with one line on the last horizontal pair. As you did at the front, note the holes across which the next line falls. Should one of the pair of horizontals go into the corner holes, the other strand goes into the first hole on each side of the back rail (figure 1.34). With the awl, gently lift up the verticals to help you get the cane through. Bending an upward hook on the last half inch of the cane will help it get through a tight spot (figure 1.35). The hook and the awl are both necessary to put the cane through in tight places.

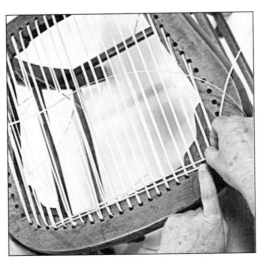

Weaving the second horizontal with the weaving end.

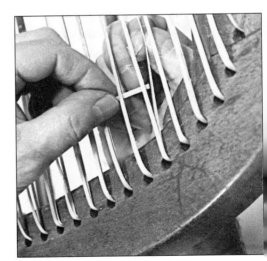

Notice how the hand on top weaves the tie end through while the other hand works from underneath to move the bottom vertical downward.

Tie off the ends on the underside as you did with the practice frame (figure 1.15). Any long ends which can make a trip across the seat can be left hanging and used to weave the diagonals.

The verticals and horizontals are now in place. Because you started the verticals in the center instead of at one edge as on the prac-

tice frame, and because you allowed half-split or fully split verticals, the curved areas at the sides are filled evenly and symmetrically. Likewise, a fully-split pair of horizontals at the front rail and again at the back rail let you maintain even spacing in the two curved areas. That is the beauty of this method: it allows easy adjustment for any odd-shaped seat.

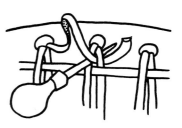

1.35 Use the awl to gently lift the verticals to get the cane through.

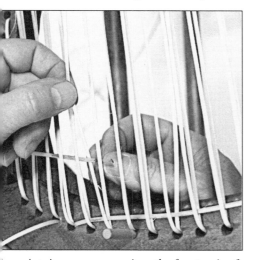

To maintain an even spacing, the front pair of horizontals on this chair is fully split. Use your paper overlay to help you make this decision (figure 1.29).

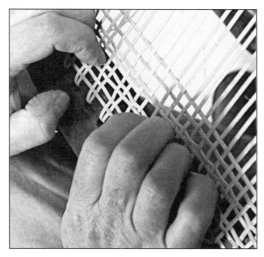

Straighten the rows with your fingernails.

Weave with opposing canes as you did on the practice frame.

A fully split pair is required in the back to accommodate the slight curve of the back rail. The first strand of the horizontal pair is woven from corner hole to corner hole; the second strand will go into the first holes on both sides of the back rail.

❖ Fixing mistakes: Cut the offending cane out of the weaving 4 inches from either side, to allow enough length for tying. Tie off the old ends, and then with a new piece of cane reweave the row. Secure this repair cane underneath as usual.

The Diagonals

❖ All the diagonals from the back left to the front right will follow the same over-under path.

Weave the diagonals the same as in the practice frame. To make the windows more distinct, dampen the whole seat with a wet cloth, and then straighten and pull the vertical and horizontal pairs closer together so the pairs are quite visible. This is heavy fingernail work. I hope you've had your gelatin. Experienced caners can find the correct windows with a minimum of straightening. You'll notice as you work that the diagonals tend to straighten the horizontals and verticals in the process of weaving.

Diagonals may be started in either rear corner and worked parallel until finished, then the second set begun. Actually, you can work both sets of diagonals simultaneously, as the two sets do not interfere with each other. Where one set goes over, the other goes under. To avoid a stacking up of loops on the bottom of the chair, often diagonals must be worked by skipping a row, then filling in the skipped row on the return trip. It is acceptable, but almost never is more than one hole skipped on the underside. Cutting a weaver for a tie simply because it does not come out

❖ Vs might occasionally be impossible to avoid where vertical and horizontal pairs are so close to the holes that Xs are impossible to make, but this is rare.

at a convenient place will produce a very unprofessional mass of knots on the underside. Planning ahead will solve this problem.

The horseshoe seat requires that you fit a square pattern into a frame with curved sides. Fishheads will play a critical role in fitting the woven interlacement into the curves of this shape. Fishheads will be opposite each other if the frame is symmetrical. On this odd shape, they will appear at the corners as well in some places along the curved side rails. As in the practice frame, Xs fall on the front, back, and sides. To help you form Xs and fishheads correctly, I suggest you familiarize yourself with the examples in figures 1.36–1.40 before beginning the diagonals. As you work, keep these illustrations close at hand for reference, and check your work as you go. Before you know it, your eye will be trained as to what to look for, and you'll be on your way to becoming a master caner.

When all the diagonals have been woven correctly, tie off the ends on the underside of the chair (figure 1.15)

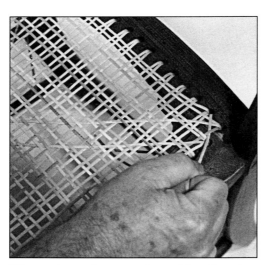

Diagonals can be woven from either direction in any order because they do not interfere with each other.

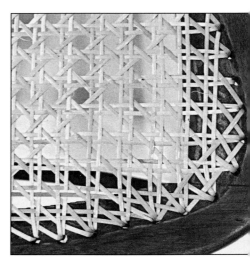

The diagonals are almost complete, There are 3 fishheads at the front curve and an X at the side.

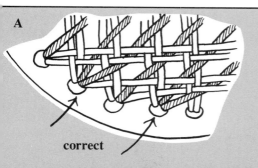

A

correct

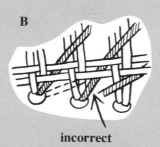

B

incorrect

incorrect

1.36 A fishhead is where two diagonals from the same direction go into the same hole. Two correct fishheads are shown in A; an incorrect fishhead is shown in B and C, where one diagonal goes to the incorrect hole.

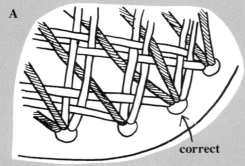

A

correct

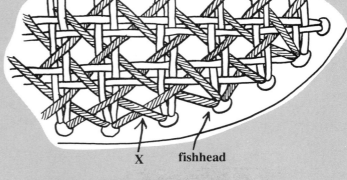

X   fishhead

1.38 The second set of diagonals completes the other half of the Xs, shown to the left of the fishhead.

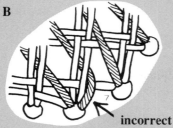

B

incorrect

1.37 Another comparison of incorrect and correct fishheads. In the incorrect example, the fishhead is not complete.

1.40 Weaving the Xs properly: if a diagonal weaves over a vertical or a horizontal, it should weave under the other arm of the X. Compare the two incorrect examples to the correct one. The arrows point at the errant canes.

correct

incorrect

incorrect

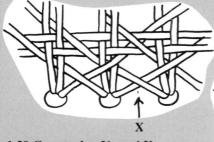

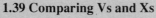

X

1.39 Comparing Vs and Xs

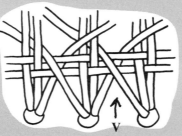

V

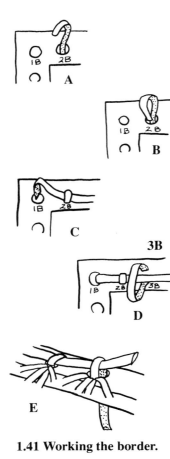

1.41 Working the border.

Working the Border

The binding, or border, covers the holes for a neat finish. Common cane ($3\frac{1}{2}$ mm wide) is normally used for binding on seats woven with Fine, Narrow Medium, or Medium cane. On seats woven with smaller cane, use Fine or Fine-Fine cane for the binding. Medium is used to weave this seat, so we'll choose Common for the binding. The binding must be held in place with lacing, which is almost always of Fine cane.

Soak a length of binding cane which is a little longer than the circumference of the edge of the caning, and several lengths of lacing cane. When both are flexible, begin the border by bringing the tie end of a length of lacing up in hole 2B, the smooth side of the cane facing out (figure 1.41A). Poke the tie end of the lacing down into the same hole, making a $\frac{1}{2}$-inch loop on the top and leaving a 4-inch tail on the underside (figure 1.41B). This first loop of lacing will hold the beginning end of the binding in place.

Make a right-angle crease pointing down, $\frac{1}{2}$ inch from one end of the binding cane. (Because the binding does not pull through any holes, it doesn't matter which end you start with.) Insert this hooked end through the $\frac{1}{2}$-inch loop of the lacing and push the bent end

of the binding down into hole 1B (figure 1.41C). Then pull the lacing tight from below. With the weaving end of the lacing, come up through hole 3B, the smooth side facing out. Loop the lacing over the binding cane, and go down the same hole with the smooth side facing out (figure 1.41D). Check with your fingers to be sure that the loop on the underside of the frame has its smooth side facing out, and then pull it tight. Then pull up on the binding on top of the back rail, holding a finger on the underside loop just tightened to keep it from sliding out. Pull down on the lacing from underneath for a final tightening (figure 1.41E). Repeat at each hole across the back rail.

Make a neat, square corner at the right back rail corner by cutting and bending the end of the binding into the corner hole. Then begin a new length of binding in the same way you started, overlapping the ends in the corner hole with no further treatment (figure 1.42). There is no lacing in the corner hole. Continue to lace the binding around the rest of the chair, making another square corner in the same way at the left back rail corner. Tie the lacing ends on the underside of the frame. The job is complete.

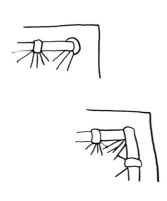

1.42 Making a neat, square corner.

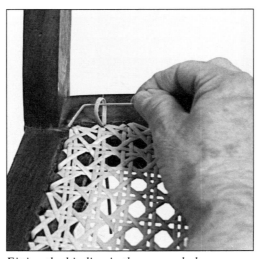

Fitting the binding in the corner hole

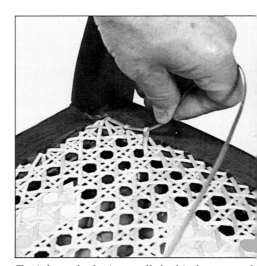

To tighten the lacing, pull the binder upwards gently while holding the lacing from below, then lower the binder and tighten the lacing.

Borders That I Don't Recommend

Some caners use permanent pegs in the corners, making their tops flush with the frame surface, but pegs are not my preference. Nor is continuing the binding cane around the corner and lacing it at the back right hole, pressing the binder into a right angle. The appearance is not neat. Binding every other hole and pegging the skipped holes does not appear finished to me (figure 1.43). Lacing every hole around the seat makes for a stronger binding and a much neater appearance.

1.43 Pegged binding. Some caners bind every other hole and peg the skipped holes.

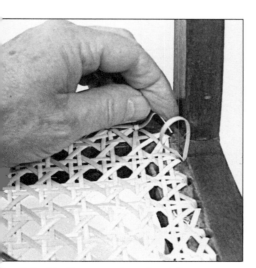

Bend the binding cane into the right corner hole.

Start the binding on the side rail by bending the end of the binder, poking it down into the corner hole. overlapping the previous binding cane.

OTHER SHAPES
Round or Egg-Shaped
(Elliptical) Seat

Like the horseshoe shape, caning for a circular frame is started at the center, and the verticals worked right and left. However, on this frame, the last pair of verticals and horizontals on each of the four "sides", front, back, left, and right, will be fully split to fill the space evenly (figure 1.44).

In an egg-shaped or elliptical seat, the layout may combine both half-split and fully-split verticals (figure 1.45). The left-hand pair shown is divided at both front and back. The pair shown next to it on the right is divided just at the back. This arrangement accommodates the sloping curve of the frame and keeps the verticals parallel. If in doubt, use the paper with parallel lines as you did in the horseshoe-shaped seat.

Keep in mind that divided canes are pairs when the horizontals or diagonals are woven across them. A single vertical or horizontal cane is never used in the layout of a regular cane pattern. In an egg-shaped seat, fishheads will appear on all four corners, and Xs fall between them on the front, back, left, and right rails. If the front "corners" look empty, a final diagonal can be woven in (figure 1.46).

Because the circular or elliptical shapes have no corners, the binding is started and ended differently than for the horseshoe shape. Start by putting the bent end of the binding cane down the center back hole. Start the lacing with the third hole (figure 1.47). Work clockwise around to the beginning. Now lace the holes skipped at the beginning, overlapping the binder for one segment. Cut the binder close to the lacing loop (figure 1.48). This method of finishing off the binder presents a continuous appearance to the border. I much prefer it to some caners' method of inserting a permanent peg to secure the binder ends in one hole.

❖ For further details about weaving these shapes, see the instructions for the balloon seat (figures 1.21-1.42).

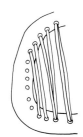

1.45 In the egg-shaped or elliptical seat, the layout may combine both half-split and fully-split verticals.

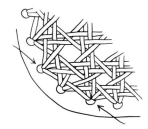

1.46 If the front "corners" look empty, a final diagonal can be woven in.

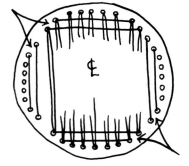

1.44 On a circular frame, the last pair of verticals and horizontals on each of the four "sides" must be fully divided to fill the spaces evenly.

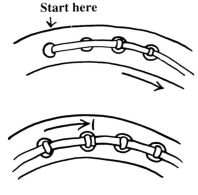

1.47 Working the binding on a circular frame.

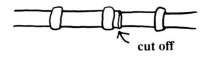

1.48 Cut the binder close to the lacing loop.

A Convex Shape

The projects considered so far have been woven in a flat plane. The next step in difficulty is to cane a three-dimensional shape, either with a convex (outward) curve as discussed here or with a concave (inward) curve as discussed in the next section.

A Lincoln rocker with a tall back and curved arms is a good example of a modest convex curve. The back post, when viewed from the side, has a shallow S curve (figure 1.49). Install the long verticals first. If the hole count across the top rail is the same as that on the bottom rail, start the verticals left and work to the right (or vice versa). If the back posts taper so there is a different number of holes at the top than at the bottom, work the verticals from the center to each side. These verticals must have less tension than used for flat work because they'll need to accommodate the three-dimensional curve. They should be only tight enough to lie more or less flat, and when depressed at midpoint

This rocker is slightly convex at the top.

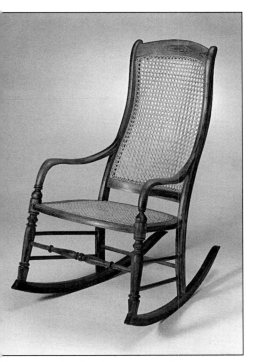

should sag about an inch. Cane is hygroscopic (absorbs water) and thus expands slightly when wet and shrinks slightly when it dries. So extra slack must be allowed in these long verticals, both for the curve and for shrinkage.

A way of ensuring that there is enough slack in the verticals is to tie a dowel or broomstick across the center of the back and weave the verticals under it. But my experience has shown that this method is completely unnecessary. If the back is deeply curved, weave the horizontals first, then the verticals. Such a rocker is mighty rare.

Start the horizontals at the bottom rail and work toward the top. Because the verticals are so long, they will tend to crowd to the center when the horizontals reach the midpoint of the back. Wet the area with a cloth or fingers and slide the verticals back into place. If the top rail is deeply curved, fit a pair (or more) of fully-split horizontals to the curve. Weave diagonals in the usual way. With parallel posts and a square bottom rail, there will be uniform Xs across the bottom and up both sides, and fishheads only at the four corners and at the top rail if it is curved.

Convex curves in cane are few except for double cane on French chairs and headboards where both the front and back are woven. As shown in figure 1.50, the cane pattern wants to pull inward and go flat. On a curved area such as this, it is important to keep the verticals firm and horizontals relaxed. Caning the outside of a cylinder would be an extreme example of a convex curve, a form unknown to me in real life. An extension of the rocker back layout, in which the frame approaches a half circle, will be discussed in the next section.

1.49 A modest convex curve on a Lincoln rocker.

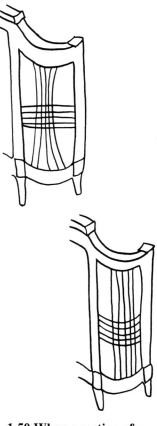

1.50 When a section of a footboard of a bed, for instance, has a pronounced outward (convex) curve the verticals must be very taut and the horizontals very relaxed or the curve will go flat. This problem will crop up in French pegged cane. By then you will be an expert and can deal with it with dispatch.

A Concave Shape

❖ There are several variations on the traditional cane pattern for drilled holes, but generally they are more decorative than practical. Usually their strength is inferior to the standard pattern. These patterns consist of one horizontal and one vertical with the usual two sets of diagonals. With the experience you have by now, you can reproduce these patterns by following the original. The Star and Lace patterns, found in the backs of fancy wicker chairs and rockers, are somewhat difficult. They are covered in two excellent sources: *Ideas for the Experienced Caner* by John and Lillian Peterka and *The Caner's Handbook* by Bruce Miller and Jim Widess (see Bibliography).

A half-circle-shaped back with a very deep curve is found on a "firehouse Windsor", a chair with a steam-bent oak frame and a cane seat and back. The seat is flat and should present no problem. The deeply curved back is more challenging. Begin weaving in the center of the back with the verticals, working to the right and then to the left. The tension should be firm, not loose, since the verticals are straight and will hold the curving horizontals in place. Near the left and right corners, some verticals will need to be split on the upper, curved rail. Remember always to keep the left vertical on top whenever you make a half-split pair (figure 1.51).

Weave the first horizontal parallel to the bottom rail. Pull it through so that it lies flat, no tighter. Either the first horizontal pair or the second or both may require splitting on both sides due to the shallow curve of the side rail at that point (figure 1.52). Keep the spacing uniform, using the lined-paper trick if you need it. When the horizontals reach the top, you'll need to use one or more split pairs to accommodate the curve.

Weave the diagonals with minimum tension, also. Even then the cane pattern will develop a saddle curve, which is normal. A tall back on a firehouse Windsor will bow out a little more because the long verticals have a little more "give". Don't make the horizontals very tight or add strong tension to the diagonals or the pattern will bow out extremely and either the verticals or the frame may break.

Put the binding on in the usual way.

A firehouse Windsor has a deeply curved concave back.

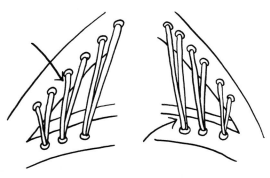

1.51 On the curved back of a firehouse Windsor, the verticals at the left and right corners will need to be split on the upper, curved rail.

1.52 On a firehouse Windsor, either the first horizontal pair or the second or both may require splitting on both sides due to the shallow curve of the side rail at this point.

FRENCH CANING

French caning is a style of hand caning that uses very narrow cane, such as Carriage and Superfine. It is often used on Louis XV and XVI, German, Italian, and bentwood furniture. While the technique for weaving French cane is the same as for larger cane sizes, the holes are more closely spaced. In addition, holes may be either blind (penetrating only part way through the frame) or through (penetrating all the way through the frame), and the verticals and horizontals may be woven with two different sizes of cane.

Because the cane is so small, French caning is more tedious and time-consuming than weaving with larger cane. If you cane for hire, be sure your charge for French caning is double that of more pedestrian jobs. French caning is not for the faint of heart, either for the caner or for the customer.

If all or part of the old cane is still in place, temporarily mark the center vertical holes and each end of the first horizontal pair with masking tape. Then with a ³/₄-inch chisel with a 30-degree taper on the blade, make short, jabbing stabs angled toward the center of the frame, and cut off the old cane flush with the top of the wood frame. Never put your other hand in the path of the blade and never aim it toward yourself. Be careful not to shave off any of the wood frame. Close attention, not great strength, is required.

With the same chisel, pull out the loops on the bottom by sliding a corner of the blade under each one. Use the awl to pry out any remaining loops. Alternatively, you can slice off loops on the bottom and pull out the seat from above, but this method doesn't work so well if the loops are in a shallow groove.

Before you begin a French cane job, be sure you have mastered regular cane. Preferably, you have long experience with regular cane. If you haven't done any caning in a while, I suggest that you review this section before beginning.

Note before removing the old chair seat whether it has been woven with two sizes of cane. Often French cane will have Carriage horizontals and verticals with Superfine or Fine-Fine diagonals. (Though not common, this same idea can also be used in larger sizes of cane.) Rarely will you find the horizontals and verticals woven in heavier cane and the diagonals in finer cane, as this arrangement sacrifices strength.

French cane on a seat in a flat plane is laid out like larger cane on an elliptical seat, but it will have more split verticals and horizontals.

Because the corner braces (knees) can't be removed, the holes at the corners will be blocked and will need to be pegged (discussion follows).

For curved work, such as the back of a barrel chair, in which the holes go all the way through the frame, lay out the job like the firehouse Windsor (page 38). Start the verticals in the center and work left and right to the side posts. Start horizontals parallel to the bottom rail and work upward. Again, keep more tension on the verticals and much less on the horizontals. Bind in the conventional manner.

PEGGED CANE

Blind holes are drilled only $5/8$ to $3/4$ inch deep without going all the way through the frame. The cane must be pegged in the holes to secure it.

Sometimes in French cane furniture, the caning forms a double wall, covering both the inside and outside of the back and the area from the arm to the seat. Other styles have a single-thickness back but double cane under the arms. While this prospect gives some caners apoplexy, the approach is perfectly straightforward. But be warned: solid experience with the larger sizes of cane is a prerequisite.

Let's start with a French cane back, pegged, with one thickness of cane. Peg proliferation is in order. Make about a hundred $1^1/4$-inch-long pegs from $3/16$-inch stock; taper one end to $1/8$ inch and the other end very slightly to $5/32$ inch. You will need one peg for every hole in the job at hand. Remove the old cane carefully with a chisel. Drill out the holes with an electric drill matching the original hole diameter. A $3/16$-inch diameter is about the maximum hole size encountered; $5/32$ or smaller may be better. Use a touch of red fingernail polish on the drill shank to serve as a depth gauge. You could go all-out with a store-bought plastic or metal depth gauge, but neither is essential. Be careful not to drill through the back and not to enlarge the holes. Vacuum out the sawdust, or hold the piece upside down and tap the frame.

Installing the Verticals in a Chair Back

Place the chair on its back on a padded table so that the top rail of the back is closest to you. Start with two wet canes, shiny side up, pegged in the rear center hole. Carefully draw the canes through your fingers, one cane on top of the other, beyond the front center hole. Clip off both canes $1/2$ to $5/8$ inch beyond the front center hole, still holding the pair taut. Bend both ends down into the hole and anchor them with a fat peg. Always keep one cane on top of the other. Since the verticals are not pulled through any holes that could tear the nodes, the direction of the cane is not important at this point.

Repeat this procedure to the left and right until all verticals are in place, dividing pairs as needed on the left and right edges. Now go back and tap the pegs in with the butt end of the awl or a small hammer. Tap enough so that the pegs are not wiggly, but not so hard that they go through the frame.

Weave horizontals from the bottom rail up. Use the weaving end of the cane to weave with at all times so that the nodes do not fray. Take the weaving end of a long strand, uncut, and weave across, leaving 2 inches extra at the far side. Trim this end to leave about $1/2$ inch beyond the hole, stick the end in the hole, and peg it (figure 1.53). At the other end, cut the cane $1/2$ inch in length, place the

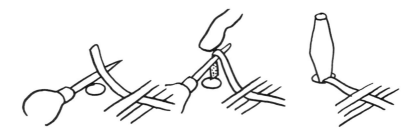

1.53 Pegging cane. Trim the excess cane to about $1/2$ inch beyond the hole, bend it over an awl, stick the end in the hole, and peg it.

end in the hole, and peg it. Use the length of cane for the next trip until the strand is used up. The awl is invaluable in putting the ends down the holes.

Weaving the Horizontals

The horizontals are woven the same as for larger sizes of cane: the first horizontal goes between the top and bottom verticals, and the second horizontal goes over the top vertical and under the bottom vertical. Place as little stress as possible on the verticals when weaving, and peg the horizontals as you go along. If a peg does not grip the cane in the hole, replace it with a fatter peg. In work left overnight, a few pegs may pop out as the cane shrinks. Replace the canes and pegs firmly and give a tap to all the others.

The cane end should be just as long as the hole is deep. If the cane is too long, trim it $1/16$ or $1/8$ inch so that maximum cane is in the hole, yet the end is not crinkled up in the bottom of the hole. Conversely, cane that is too short in the hole will not allow the peg to grip it firmly. Strict attention to this small point is critical. Hole depth less than $1/2$ inch makes this operation difficult; $5/8$ inch is nearly ideal; and $3/4$ inch is even better if the frame thickness permits.

A heavy hand, a weight, or a cat in the center of the chair back at this point is a no-no. The prospect of starting over is not a happy one.

The Diagonals

Weave the diagonals as usual. Adding the cane ends of the diagonals to the holes will make them even more crowded. If necessary, use the smaller end of the peg to anchor the cane.

One advantage of pegged cane is that you are working with short lengths of cane; you don't have to pull 15 feet through each time you weave across. Another advantage is that you can use cane scraps for some of the shorter verticals, horizontals, or diagonals, or as lacing for the binding. File your scraps in separate piles according to width (Superfine, Fine-Fine, and Fine).

Working the Border

There are several ways to work the border; the method shown here is the conventional way and probably the original technique. Choose binding cane that is the same width as the diagonals or slightly larger, but narrower than the hole diameter. Measure a length of binding cane to go around the work plus 4 or 5 inches, assuming that the border is continuous. The lacing in pegged cane is not a continuous strand as it is in caning with through holes, but it is a plug, a short piece shaped like a paper clip. To make these plugs, cut pieces of Fine-Fine cane about $1 1/4$ inches long. Soak it well before beginning so that it will bend easily.

To bind a chair back, lay the chair on a low table so that the back is horizontal. Pull out six or eight pegs in the bottom center of the chair back, and place a $1/8$-inch drop of Elmers Glue-All® or other white glue on the cane side of all but holes 1 and 2 (figure 1.54A). There is no need to fill the holes with glue, nor should there be too little. Bend down the starting end of the binding cane and put it down hole 1 (figure 1.54A). Fold one of the lacing plugs and insert it over the binding cane (figure 1.54B) into a hole with glue. Push it firmly down with a short $1/4$-inch-diameter dowel or the smooth side of side-cutting pliers. This is a delicate maneuver; it will be easier if one leg of the plug is a little longer than the other. Insert the longer leg first, then the shorter one over the binder into the hole. Repeat with the other glued holes, then remove another six pegs, add glue, and repeat until you reach the beginning. After completing a section of half a dozen holes, go back and push the plugs down again. If a loop still sticks up, either ream the hole with the awl or cut a shorter plug. At the last two holes (numbers 1 and 2 in figure 1.54A), overlap the binder for one segment and glue in these two plugs. Cut off the binder very close to the last plug (figure 1.55).

Allow at least an hour for the glue to set; overnight is even better. Until it's set, don't stress the back.

Another binding method I sometimes use to match an existing border is to peg all the

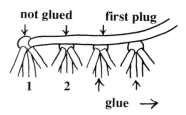

1.54A **Starting the binding cane.**

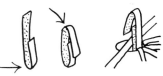

1.54 B **Cut cane plugs for the binding. Place a $1/8$-inch drop of glue on the cane side of each hole. Fold a short piece of cane, insert it over the binding cane into a hole, and push it firmly down.**

1.55 **Cut off the binder very close to the last plug.**

1.56 For a binding that is permanently pegged, cut pieces of binding cane about 1¹/₄ to 1¹/₂ inches long and bend each like a staple. Apply a spot of glue to each hole and secure the cane with matchstick pegs.

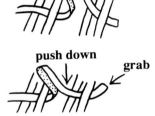

push down   **grab**

1.57 Working two layers of cane. Turn up the weaving end of the damp cane to make a hook. With one hand, move the verticals slightly as needed, and work with the hooked cane in the other hand, holding it only 1 or 2 inches from the end.

1.58 When working from one side of the cane only, depress the bottom vertical with your finger and push the cane through with the other hand.

holes permanently. Cut pieces of binding cane 1¹/₄ to 1¹/₂ inches long. Insert one leg in a hole and the other leg in the next hole. Repeat for six holes. With the ³/₄-inch chisel held vertically, cut wooden kitchen matches into ¹/₂-inch lengths, discarding the heads. Apply a spot of glue to each hole and push the matchstick pegs in with a short length of dowel or a small hammer (figure 1.56). A snug fit is required.

DOUBLE-PEGGED CANE

Double-pegged caning is two layers of pegged cane; its disadvantage is that one hand cannot work on the underside of the cane. You'll find that making a "hook" at the end of the weaving end of your cane is indispensable. This is definitely not the place for the beginner to begin. Basic layout, cane handling, and working with curved frames in three dimensions are all foundation skills that you should master first.

Let's start with a chair where the holes are all blind on the inside underarm panel and independent of those on the outside panel. If possible, remove the cane from both the inside and outside of the arms. Weave the inside panel first while you still have the luxury of working with one hand on the other side. Where cane goes over the wood frame at the edges, use the awl to lift and slide the cane underneath. In tight corners, you can pull out pegs adjacent to the working area to weave the cane in, and then replace them when finished. Be sure the pegs holding the vertical strands are kept firmly in place.

Once the diagonals are in and the binder installed, begin the outside panel. Installing the verticals will not be difficult, but the horizontals will prove challenging since weaving can be done from just one side. Turn up the weaving end of the damp cane to make a hook. With one hand, move the verticals slightly as needed, and work with the hooked cane in the other hand (figure 1.57), holding it only 2 or 3 inches from the end. On the first horizontal row of a pair, you can weave without a hook. Make the weaving end flat, and slide it under the top vertical and over the

Some styles, such as French Provincial furniture, have no binding at all. Glue matchstick pegs in the holes without binding cane. If the matchsticks are too small, use round rattan of the correct diameter cut to ¹/₂-inch lengths with a sharp chisel to make square ends.

lower vertical, depressing the bottom vertical about ¹/₈ inch with your finger (figure 1.58). After you've made three or four stitches, pull the cane through. A cane length is only as long as the width of the woven panel plus 2 inches. You can weave every horizontal from the same direction to accommodate your left- or right-handedness. Three or four rows can be woven before you go back to trim and peg the ends.

As you near the top of the panel, the weaving will get progressively tighter and you will have to use the awl to make space. By now you will be adept at spotting skipped stitches, maybe even before they are formed. They will set off red rockets and loud alarms. With practice, this method goes fairly fast. Weave the diagonals, also using the "hook", and glue in the binder as usual.

When replacing an inside panel while the outside panel of cane is to remain intact, the procedure is the same. Do all the weaving from the front. Working conditions are apt to be crowded, but if you have progressed this far, I am confident you can do it.

OTHER SPECIAL TECHNIQUES

Double Hand Cane, Not Pegged

Some chairs have a double layer of cane on a frame that has through holes. On these, the hand caning goes through the holes to weave both sides. One style I encountered was a Hepplewhite armchair with rectangular panels under the arms, the inside and outside panels spaced $1/2$ inch apart. Another was a cane back on a mahogany chair from the passenger ship *Bremen*, now scrapped.

On this type of chair, begin with the verticals but work both sides at the same time by taking the cane around and around front to back through the holes. Loops will alternate on both sides of the frame. Similarly, weave the horizontals across the inside, through the hole, and across the outside, using the hook on the end of the cane to help you weave. Ends cannot be tied, so leave them sticking out and temporarily pegged. As work progresses, the new loops help to bind the ends in the holes. Diagonals go around from front to back also. Try to distribute the back loops as evenly as possible. This requires a bit of planning and skill, as does weaving the diagonals without missing a row. As a last resort, fill in a missing row with a short cane, and tuck the end down the hole as in pegged cane. The back loops look like a binder and no other binder is required, except where bare wood shows between holes. For a uniform appearance, glue in a U-shaped piece of cane to cover the wood. To finish the job, closely cut off all tails with a sharp knife and apply a spot of glue to canes that won't stay down. Permanent matchstick pegs are best dispensed with, as they push out the tails on the other side.

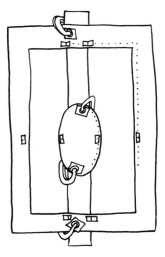

1.59 Securing a medallion on a chair back. Temporarily fix the medallion in place with a board and clamps. Check that the space is equal left and right, and that the horizontal marks on the frame and medallion line up.

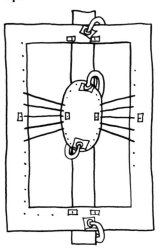

1.60 Weaving a medallion. Starting with the matching horizontal axis holes marked with tape, work the radial cane pairs alternately on the left and the right. Then work alternately up and down from the horizontal line until you reach the clamped board.

Hand-Caned Suspended Medallion

Considered the ultimate challenge by some, the suspended plaque with radial cane is no more difficult than double cane and uses the same basic cane pattern, albeit with distortions. Before removing the old cane, mark the center horizontal axis with small pieces of masking tape, one hole on each outside edge of the plaque and the corresponding holes on the frame (figure 1.59). Mark the vertical axis in the same way.

Carefully remove the old cane and clean the holes with a drill. Temporarily fix the medallion in place with a board and clamps. Use a soft pine 1-by-2 long enough to span the vertical axis of the back with a little overhang. Center it vertically on the chair back and clamp it, protecting the chair with small cloth pads. You can make centering easier by sticking bits of masking tape 1 inch on either side of the centerline of the outer frame; put marks on the plaque as well. Clamp the medallion to the board (figure 1.59) with small clamps (larger ones will get in the way). Check to see that the space is equal left and right and that the horizontal marks on the frame and medallion line up. Some caners use string in place of the clamps to suspend the medallion temporarily, but I find it's like working with Jello and will ensure that the medallion gets cocked.

Whether the holes are all drilled through, all pegged, or the outside frame is pegged and the medallion drilled through, the layout is the same. Two-strand radials correspond to the vertical pairs in regular caning, and the "horizontals" weave in circles around and around the medallion. Starting with the matching horizontal axis holes marked with tape, work the radial cane pairs alternately on the left and the right (figure 1.60). Keep the tension as even as possible and continue working alternately up and down from the horizontal line until the clamped board forces a stop. If you are working with through holes, make the ends terminate on the outside frame at this point. If you are working with pegged cane, be sure the kitchen matchstick pegs are firmly stuck in place. You will glue them in

Chair back with a hand-caned suspended medallion.

permanently when the caning is complete. Remove the clamps and board, and fill in the rest of the radials.

Examine the old cane to determine how many pairs of "horizontals" you will need. Weave the first pair at the correct spacing out from the medallion, starting and ending the cane by overlapping the ends $1^1/_2$ to 2 inches (figure 1.61). Stagger these overlaps in the lower part of the chair back (figure 1.62). As overlaps will not stay on top of one another, let them sit side by side for now, leaving a $^1/_2$-inch tail sticking out to use as a handle later. Continue concentric pairs of cane working out to the frame, paying close attention to the spacing.

An alternative to concentric ovals is weaving in a continuous spiral, starting in the center below the plaque. Even though the result is much the same as the concentric pattern, the beginning and end are quite visible (to me) and the layout is not as neat as the first method.

If the holes in the medallion are large enough to allow you to weave diagonals directly into them, proceed with the diagonals, keeping all tie ends on the outside frame. Because the holes are close together on the tight curve of the oval, the area above and below the medallion will be crowded. If you choose a wider cane for the diagonals, be sure it is not so wide as to prevent weaving in this crowded area.

Some medallions will not permit diagonals woven directly into them because the holes are too small and closely spaced. In this case, the radials alone support the medallion, and the weaving is spaced out 1 to 2 inches away from it. Weave the diagonals from the frame to the inside cane pair, then turn back and go to the outside frame (figure 1.63). The cane must be wet to make this abrupt turn. The radial pair will be pinched together by the diagonal canes as they make this turn. This will give the appearance of one radial cane going to each hole in the medallion; they will be very close together as they converge on the medallion and will spread apart as they go toward the outside frame of the chair back. The area around the medallion where the radials converge on it will have gaps between the radials. Often this area between the medallion and the first row of weaving is filled with three or four rows of cane woven over and under the radials like the inner rings of Saturn. This "collar" is just decorative, and satisfies an urge to fill empty spaces. Your eye and your urges will be the judge of whether to add a collar (1.64).

The diagonals will hold the horizontal overlaps in place. Drag wet fingers across the splice to dampen it, and slide one end on top of the other, using the small tail and the awl to help coax them into place. Add a spot of white glue to secure them and trim off the tails, front and back.

Bind the outer frame as appropriate. Smaller wooden matches, from a pocket-size box, may be just right to peg the medallion; it usually has no binding.

❖ Before removing the old cane, check the correspondence of the medallion holes with the holes in the frame. Some holes may need double pairs and some may need single pairs.

1.61 Starting and ending the cane by overlapping the ends 1¹/₂ to 2 inches.

1.62 Stagger overlaps in the lower part of the chair back.

1.63 If the holes of a medallion are too small and closely spaced to hold the diagonals, weave them from the frame to the inner horizontal pair, then turn back and go to the outer frame.

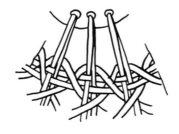

1.64 Weaving a collar between the medallion and the woven web.

Bentwood

European bentwood is made from steam-bent beech, often with dramatic curlicues. Some American furniture makers have used oak or occasionally walnut. The originator of the process was the Viennese firm Gebrüder Thonet (pronounced like Bonnet with a T). You'll find the Thonet name burned into the wood on the underside of the seats; paper labels which often fell off were also used. Modern-day imitators of these traditional chairs are manufactured in Czechoslovakia, Poland, Italy, and Spain. Most older bentwood pieces and some high-quality modern ones are hand caned. Many recent ones are machine caned because of the high cost of labor.

Bentwood frames for hand caning have deep grooves to conceal the cane loops on the back side or underside. Knots are impossible to tie, so the tail ends are simply cut off. Binding is laced as usual or glued in as for pegged cane (glue is better because it holds the cane in place). Exposed backs often have spline set into the groove. Once the caning is completed, replace the spline, which was destroyed when you removed it, with a suitable rattan spline such as is used in machine caning (see page 51). Place glue on both sides of the groove, clamp the spline in place if necessary. When the glue is completely dry, shave the spline off flush, sand, and finish. If a chair has a beechwood spline that is almost invisible, it may be desirable to leave it intact and peg the handwoven cane from the front, taking great care not to drill through the spline when you clean the holes.

Bentwood chairs are joined with screws and large lag bolts which are easily removed. It is best to take out the seat or back frame to cane it.

PLASTIC CANE

Some customers insist on using plastic cane because of its supposed longer wearing qualities. However, I feel that it is far better to use the genuine article from the beginning. I find that plastic looks like what it is, an offense to the eye, and sags considerably under a warm behind. My argument is that an owner who can afford a fine chair can afford to repair it with real cane. Plastic cane in a fine walnut chair is a sad sight.

FINISHING HAND CANE

Hairs on the finished cane provoke tizzies in some caners. Trim the worst of them off with small side-cutting pliers. The rest will wear off in a short time. If you wish to live dangerously, they can be singed off with a blowtorch or a gas flame. But I don't want to hear you say, "Oops," or worse as your work disappears.

I prefer no finish at all on cane. However, here are some techniques used by other caners.

Some caners advocate monthly applications of water, which simulate for an hour desirable humid conditions. The trouble is, the moisture is gone in an hour, and the cane is back exactly where it was before. Moisture is also used to shrink a sagging seat, but the results are slight and temporary. The sag comes back.

The least damaging finish for cane is wax; use paste wax or a mixture of beeswax and turpentine, one of the oldest finishes of all. You can make it easily by putting pea-size pellets of beeswax in a small jar of turpentine with a tight lid, using about $1/3$ beeswax to $2/3$ turpentine. If it congeals in cold weather, warm it up but not on a stove, as it is quite flammable. A commercial mixture much like it is Hagerty's Vernax, which is available in many hardware stores. Beeswax polish gives a soft sheen to fine wood and can be used to buff the canework as well. Wax accelerates a fine golden patina, which cane acquires anyway without help from anyone.

If you need to use stain to match an existing chair, oil stain is best. After staining, leave it to dry for several days, then glaze the chair seat with a thin coat of white or orange 3-lb-cut shellac. Varnish and lacquer make cane dry and brittle, though in commercial operations everything is lacquered these days because it is economical. Most objectionable is a white reproduction French antique with the cane drenched in white lacquer; its beautiful cane will fail in a short time. If you are faced with replacing and matching color in such a seat, try to match the color with artist's acrylic colors thinned with water. Two coats should do. The cane will sag from the damp but will shrink back when dry. When it's completely dry, glaze the seat with a thin coat of shellac. Artist's oil colors will work well, too, but take longer to dry.

If you need to imitate a fine splattering of dots found on the original chair, do it after the stain or color is dry but before you shellac the seat. Use a 1-inch brush with medium thick,

oil-base paint in the tip of the brush. Hold the brush about a foot away from the cane surface and flip the end of the bristles. Wipe the frame free of straying dots. When the dots are dry, shellac the seat.

Remember, the least you do to cane benefits it the most. However, if you must do something to increase the longevity of a caned chair seat, a thin cushion will increase the mileage considerably.

Working with cane brings the caner into contact with the fancy chairs of the first half of the nineteenth century that featured stenciling, gilding, and pinstriping. Sheraton and Hitchcock styles, among others, display elaborate and colorful examples. The bibliography lists two excellent works on decorating these chairs, one by Brazer and the other by Lea. These techniques are almost a lost art, though you sometimes see them applied to automobiles.

Useful Colors in Oil Stain:
HONEY MAPLE: medium tan. Can be thinned with turpentine for a pale tint. AMERICAN WALNUT: dark brown. Can be darkened with lampblack (artist's oil) for brownish-black. Two coats may be necessary to darken the color on the cane.

PATCHING HAND CANE

Sometimes cane can be patched to avoid redoing the whole job. Generally this is practical only where the area is small, less than an inch square, or is confined to a few strands. Generally patching is not feasible if the original cane is old and brittle and breaks as fast as you weave; the cane is heavily painted with varnish, lacquer, or paint, which glue the strands together; or the breaks are at the edges, where the cane joins the frame.

Although patching is often a dubious economy, the caner must include it in his or her arsenal of techniques. Repair horizontals and

verticals first, overlaying the original cane with an overlap of two or three stitches on each end (figure 1.65). Make the stitches one at a time or you risk pulling out the weaver. Repair the diagonals last. Leave 2-inch tails on everything, and then use them and the awl to straighten the cane. When the patch is completed and all canes straightened, clip closely all tails and any broken ends on the back. Apply small dots of glue to the cane ends, front and back, and smooth them out with a finger.

1.65 Repair broken canes by weaving in replacement cane over the original, overlapping for two or three stitches on each end. Here the patched cane is woven through and then slid on top of the horizontal to be repaired.

HOW TO DRILL HOLES IN A CHAIR SEAT FOR HAND CANING

1.66 Establishing the hole placement on a rectangular seat.

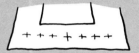

front

A. Lay out the front holes.

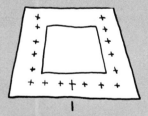

B. Lay out the side holes so that they line up with the left and right front corner holes.

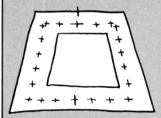

C. Lay out the back row. If the back corner holes do not coincide, redraw the lines on the left and right rails.

Drilling holes in a chair not previously caned is easily accomplished. The basic element is a square grid laid on the seat frame. For a rectangular seat such as an oak pressed-back chair with broad, flat rails, the layout is done directly on the wood. Using a colored lead pencil and ruler, draw a line on the front rail, $^3/_4$ inch from the inner edge of the seat. (Setting this line only $^1/_2$ inch in risks splitting the wood when the caning stress is applied.) Mark the centers front and back. Choose a hole spacing from Appendix B, and mark off the spaces from the center to the left and right on the front rail, making a pencil tick at each point. Draw lines down the side rails from the corner points, approximating the $^3/_4$-inch distance from the inner seat edge and mark the hole spacing on these lines. Repeat for the back rail, starting the markings at the center. The moment of truth is at the corners, which may require you to shift the lines on the side rails so that the corner ticks coincide (figure 1.66). Once the points are established, tap the awl at each point to make a dent for the drill. Drill holes from the top, straight through the wood. Shave off the splinters on the bottom with the $^3/_4$-inch chisel.

A round or elliptical seat is more complicated. Tape a sheet of $^1/_4$-inch squared paper large enough to cover the seat, center line to center line. Trace roughly the inner four edges of the frame. Remove the paper from the seat, and on it draw a line parallel to, and $^3/_4$ inch outside, the tracing line, improving on the curve if needed. Mark the hole points on each side of the midpoint, front and back with dividers, leaving about a 30- to 40-degree quadrant empty on the four "corners". Make the spacing $^1/_{32}$ to $^1/_{16}$ inch larger and mark the quadrants. Use the original spacing to mark the left and right sides, being sure that the marks are directly opposite each other on the left and right. There will be a good amount of juggling and fudging to make them fit. It is easier to do this on the squared paper than to do it on the wood frame. There must be no odd single point, since each point must have a mate opposite it. When this positioning is finished, tape the template to the frame, lined up exactly, and tap the awl at each point through the paper into the wood. Remove the paper and drill. Hole layout has to be careful and exact: successful caning depends on it (figure 1.67).

Pegged cane with blind holes offers more freedom in layout, as these holes can be drilled almost anywhere, provided the wood frame is strong enough to support the cane's tension. But the holes must still be based on a square grid, whatever the frame shape.

1.67 Making a layout on squared paper for a round or elliptical seat. Slightly increase the spacing on the quadrant, the area that would be the corner of a square seat.

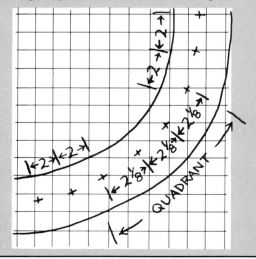

MACHINE CANE
CHAPTER II

A pressed-back chair with a machine-caned seat. Courtesy of Tole House
Antiques.

Materials
Tools
Machine caning a
    rectangle
Variations
    A barrel chair
Suspended medallion
Other materials

Cane webbing, also known as machine cane or pressed cane, is a commercially woven cane mesh that is inserted into a groove around a chair seat in imitation of the traditional hand technique. It is not, as one of my customers thought, raveled at the edges and then the ends stuck down through drilled holes.

Machine cane began to be used about 1900, when labor costs for handwoven cane became prohibitively expensive. By using machine cane, factories could mass-produce chairs with "genuine cane seats" at a fraction of the cost of hand-caned chairs. Hand-caned chairs were still readily available during this period: Sears, Roebuck and Montgomery Ward catalogs offered hand-caned dining chairs for 98¢ each. Today, nearly all modern caned furniture uses machine cane. Some exceptions are fine furniture imported from Italy, Spain, and Brazil.

From the end of World War II until the 1950s, when labor costs became prohibitive, cane web was woven in Germany. Today it is woven in Singapore and Hong Kong. It is made in two steps. First, pairs of verticals (warp) and horizontals (weft) are machine woven on power looms. This fabric becomes the base for the diagonals, which are woven in by hand using a long, corkscrewlike wire that holds a cane strand fastened to its tip. By rotating the other end of this tool, the wire caner turns the strand through the "windows" in the webbing to the far side.

Machine cane is available in a variety of sizes, patterns, and widths (figure 2.1—see Appendix C for a more complete listing). Widths range from 12 to 36 inches. You can

Materials consist of scissors or shears, a 1/8-inch chisel, a 3/4-inch chisel, knife, Elmer's Glue-All®, a medium-sized hammer or dead-blow hammer, a tapered maple wedge, a square-edged maple block, cane, and spline.

urchase machine cane by the foot (relatively xpensive) or by the roll (usually 50 feet ong). Not all patterns are available in all vidths.

MATERIALS

In choosing machine cane for a specific eat, keep in mind that the smaller, finer veaves are more fragile than the larger ones. he finer weaves are usually installed on hair backs. Radio Net and Swedish Modern two styles of cane web that do not have hand-voven diagonals) are sometimes used on eats, but they are not as strong or durable as ane with diagonals. The cane size used for most purposes is $1/2$-inch mesh standard cane vith diagonals.

Rattan spline is used in machine caning to old the cane webbing in place in the groove. t is available in graduated sizes (figure 2.2). Choose the size that fits loosely in the empty, leaned-out groove. If the spline is too small, t will not make a friction fit in the groove to eep the cane webbing in place. If it's too arge, it will protrude above the frame surface.

TOOLS

A few special tools are needed to remove he old spline and cane. Chisels with stout hafts are required; get chisels with blade

$1/2$-inch mesh

Swedish modern, medium

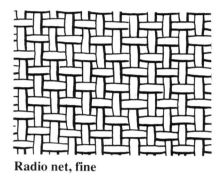
Radio net, fine

Close-woven, medium

2.1 Some of the different types of machine cane webbing.

2.2 Choose a size of spline that fits the groove easily.

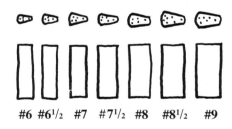
#6 #6$1/2$ #7 #7$1/2$ #8 #8$1/2$ #9

❖ Substitution of round rattan in place of regular spline is another aberration. It does not grip the groove properly and usually falls out.

#9$1/2$ #10 #10$1/2$ #11 #12

pline should fit loosely in the groove.

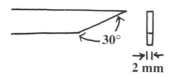

2.3 A 2 mm chisel ground to a 30-degree taper.

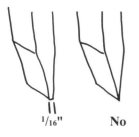

2.4 Taper wedges to $^1/_{16}$ inch.

2.5 The best knife for trimming is a modified chip-carving knife. Round off the cutting edge with a grindstone.

widths of $^1/_8$ inch, 2 mm, and 3 mm. A narrow chisel with a curved shaft, a type used for lathework, is useful where curved grooves are encountered. A $^3/_4$-inch chisel serves to cut the cane off the chair and also to cut the spline. Each chisel should be ground to a 30-degree taper; use a 2- or 3-inch-diameter medium stone in an electric drill to grind a shallow, hollow-ground long taper (figure 2.3). Finish the edge by hand on a fine oilstone. Remember: sharp tools are imperative; dull ones quadruple the work. Keep your chisels razor sharp by honing them on a fine oilstone after each use. If you are unable to find a $^1/_8$-inch chisel, you can make do by grinding down a $^1/_4$-inch chisel to $^1/_8$, provided that you don't draw the temper. Marples, an English brand of chisels, is suitable (see Suppliers in Appendix A).

You'll need to make wooden wedges for forcing the machine cane into the groove. Cut six 1-by-3-inch rectangles from $^1/_8$-inch maple stock with the grain running the long way. With the $^3/_4$-inch chisel, taper one nar-

row end of each block to $^1/_{16}$ inch (figure 2.4). Make two more blocks, each $^1/_{16}$ by 1 by 3 inches, with squared edges, to push the spline down in the groove. For tapping the wedges, I use a dead-blow hammer (a rubber mallet with shot in the end), though a rubber mallet or ordinary hammer will do.

For trimming the cane around the chair seat, modify the straight blade of a chip-carving knife (available from Woodcraft) by grinding it into a curve. Hold the tip against a medium or coarse grindstone until the shape resembles the one in figure 2.5. Finish by grinding both sides of the cutting edge and then honing them on a fine stone to a razor-sharp edge. This knife has an excellent handle, and the small, maneuverable blade is well suited to machine cane. It is also good for tapping pegs in hand caning. Single-edged razor blades are a poor substitute; they are hard to hold and are a menace to the user. You'll also need a white glue such as Elmer's Glue-All® to secure the cane in the groove.

MACHINE CANING A RECTANGLE

The simplest shape to begin with is a recti-linear seat, with parallel front and back rails and sides that angle (slope) slightly to the back, such as are found on many pressed-back chairs from the early part of this century.

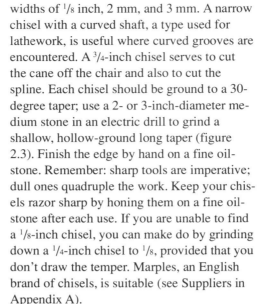

A completed machine-caned seat.

Removing the Old Cane

With the $^3/_4$-inch chisel, shave off the old cane and any protruding spline. Slice off all that extends above the wood surface, being careful not to scratch or gouge the frame. *Always aim the chisel away from you, and never put the other hand in front of the chisel when it is in use.* As good caners are hard to find, let's not self-destruct. After you have removed the old cane, clean out the groove by pushing the narrow chisel down firmly into the spline $^1/_2$ inch back from the front corner and working toward the back. Angle the chisel at about 30 to 40 degrees to make a sloping cut. Lower the handle to pry out a chip, but don't apply too much power or you will break the shaft of the chisel. If you can buy or make a deep chisel, insert the point near the bottom of the groove and lift with a rocking motion. Most of the spline should come out. Otherwise, continue to pry out segments with the narrow chisel. After most of the spline is out, pry out the $1/2$ inch of spline at the corner. Always work the corners with the chisel pointing into the corner and away from yourself. Next, with the flat side of the chisel blade held against the side of the groove, shave off the remaining spline and cane on the inner and outer sides of the groove. Avoid taking chunks out of the frame. Finally, clean out the bottom of the groove. Rotate the handle slightly as you slide the taper side of the chisel along the bottom, giving it a wiggle, to clean out the rest of the cane. Do the other three sides the same way.

A difficult situation for the caner is the curved spline on a rear rail with a vertical splat sitting on it. The following method is useful. With a sharp $3/4$-inch chisel, attack from the top (figure 2.6A). Push the chisel down in the crack between the inner side of the groove and the spline. Use only hand pressure on the chisel. Pry out the spline a splinter at a time. With the flat of the blade against the outer side of the groove (figure 2.6B), push the blade straight down to loosen the remaining spline. Return to the inner side of the groove. With the flat of the blade against the inner side, slice straight down to remove the remaining spline and cane. Final cleanup is with a curved chisel (figure 2.6C).

Carefully remove the old cane and spline with the $1/8$-inch chisel.

Spline removal is frequently a difficult job which requires a digression to discuss its problems and possible solutions. Two types of glue are commonly used, hide glue and white glue. Before white glue came into use, hide glue was used in most furniture construction. Spline secured with old hide glue normally pops right out, the glue being dry and crumbling. If the chair has been dipped to remove the finish, the glue is practically gone. Not so with white glue; once set, it can't be made to go back to a liquid state. Some have tried soaking the glue with vinegar or a 5 percent solution of acetic acid, but in my experience, the vinegar merely makes the spline swell tighter, a most unwelcome result. The sticky mess on the wood finish is unwelcome also, not to mention the pickle factory smell. I prefer to chisel out the spline by hand, absolutely dry.

Some people have used a router to clean out the groove, but I don't recommend this method. For one thing, the router's soleplate comes into contact with the back posts and arms. The solution is to disassemble the chair completely, so that the seat is a flat plane. Another problem is that it is impossible to hold a router steady to cut a straight line, freehand, and then negotiate a 1- or 2-inch radius at the corner of the frame. Deviations from the original groove are disastrous. Don't even think of trying this method. Others have used a Mototool and Foredom fitted with a burr or small saw to remove spline by turning it into sawdust. It works, but takes forever. The chisel is more efficient, gives better control, and produces the least damage.

While rattan spline is relatively soft, occasionally you'll find a chair with hard maple spline. Use a very sharp, narrow chisel with the strongest shaft. Begin in the center and pound the chisel in with a hammer to remove the spline a chip at a time. After pressure has been relieved in the center, the sides of the spline can be pried out. When a whole stick pops out, it's cause for celebration. This isn't an easy job; I charge extra to remove hard maple spline.

2.6 Removing spline around a vertical splat.

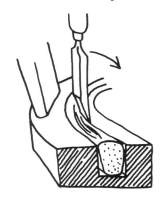

A. From the top, push the chisel down into the crack between the inner side of the groove and the spline. Remove the spline a splinter at a time.

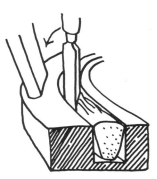

B. Loosen the remaining spline by using the flat side of the blade against the outer edge of the groove.

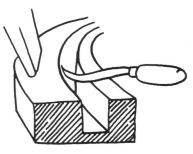

C. Clean out the groove with a curved chisel.

Installing the New Cane

With all of the spline out, clean the groove with a small vacuum or invert the chair and tap the bottom of the seat. Check the inner edge of the seat frame. If it is not rounded, ease it with a file or shave $^1/_{16}$ inch off with the $^3/_4$-inch chisel. This prevents the cane from being sheared off when sat on. On backs it is not necessary. The easier job of installing the cane can now begin.

Cut the new piece of machine cane to reach 1 inch beyond the groove on each side. If the old cane seat is intact, you can use it for a pattern. Place the cane webbing in a tub or a small plastic swimming pool of lukewarm water. After 15 to 20 minutes, remove it and blot it with a towel.

It is not necessary to soak spline for rectangular seats or for gentle curves, but it is essential to soak it to make it pliable for small shapes or radii of 3 inches or less. Put the spline in to soak with the cane webbing and leave it in the water while you install the cane. Heavy spline needs to soak 30 minutes or more. You'll know when it is ready for use when you can bend it easily without its breaking or cracking.

Center the cane on the seat frame. With a wedge and the hammer, tap down the rear center area into the groove for 3 to 4 inches. At the front, align the cane pattern with the inner edge of the frame, or with the joins where the side rails meet the front rail. The center part of the seat should lie reasonably flat. Stretching the cane is not necessary because it will shrink tight as it dries, in two to three hours.

Tap the cane down in the center front for 4 to 6 inches. If the cane is not aligned with the frame, pull it up and reposition it. Return to the back and finish tapping the cane down, working to the corners. At the front, tap down the remaining cane the same way.

Do the sides next, working back to front on alternate sides. Tap lightly—the wedge might go completely through the cane if you hit it too hard. The object is to push the cane into the groove in a U shape; that's why it's called "pressed" cane. The cane will be damp enough to work for an hour; an average job takes 10 to 15 minutes.

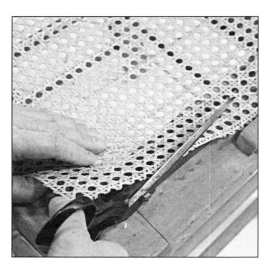

Place soaked cane over the chair seat and trim it with a 1-inch margin all around.

With a wooden wedge and mallet, begin tapping the cane into the groove in the center of the back of the seat.

✤ Some caning manuals give the following sequence: install cane, put in spline, and trim cane; but I find the result sloppy. Trimming the cane first, before installing the spline, provides a neat outer join which shows professional skill.

t the front, straighten the cane pattern so
'hat it is parallel to the front groove or the
'ont inside edge of the seat frame. Tap the
'ane into the center of the front groove.
'lternately tap to the left and right up to the
'orners. Do the same for the back groove.

*Starting at a back corner, tap the cane into
the side grooves, working alternately on the
right and left.*

Trimming the Cane

Cut off the surplus cane sticking up on the utside of the groove with the knife. Cut just elow the top outside edge of the groove. Hold the knife up to prevent cutting the cane n the inside edge of the groove (figure 2.7). Keep a firm grip on the knife and slice slowly

and deliberately, being careful not to slip. Gently pull the surplus cane away as you cut. If it does not let go, slice lightly again. Trim the corners by pressing the knife firmly against the cane, like a guillotine. Remove all of the cane scraps from the groove.

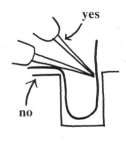

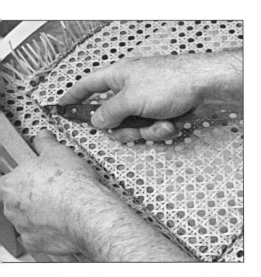

*Holding the 1-inch margin of cane flat on the
surface of the seat with your thumb, grasp the
knife in your other hand. Firmly, steadily, and
slowly cut the cane just below the outer edge
of the groove.*

2.7 After installing the cane, trim off the excess. Cut just below the top edge of the groove, keeping the knife up and away from the webbing.

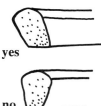

yes

no

45°

2.8 Cut the spline at 45 degrees, with an undercut.

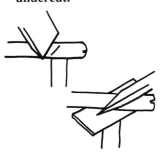

2.9 At the corner, mark the crown of the spline with a chisel. Place the spline on your wood block and cut at a 45-degree angle with an undercut.

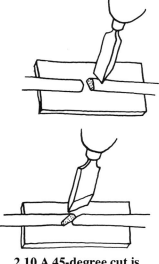

2.10 A 45-degree cut is neater than a 90-degree butt join.

Securing the Cane With Spline

Run a $1/8$-inch bead of white glue all around on the *cane* side of the groove. Working on a hard surface and starting from the top or crown side, cut one end of the spline at a 45-degree angle with an undercut (figure 2.8). Place the narrow underside of the spline in a corner of the groove. Tap it into the groove with the mallet, working from the cut end and stopping 3 inches from the next corner.

For a chair with a square corner, miter the spline. Looking straight down from the top, mark the spline at the corner with the chisel, making a light cut on the crown. Slide the flat side of the maple tapping block under the spline and use a chisel to cut a 45-degree angle, with an undercut (figure 2.9). Tap down the end into the corner. This undercut enables the crowns of the splines to meet at the corners in a hairline join.

The 45-degree join looks much better than a 90-degree butt join (figure 2.10). Cutting

45s is an eyeball affair; if the joint doesn't fit, the spline can be quickly recut. Rock the chisel back and forth to facilitate this cut (figure 2.11).

To add the next piece of spline, cut a 45-degree angle in the opposite direction and fit this to the corner just completed (figure 2.12). Press the end into the corner and tap it down, continuing along the right side of the seat. Repeat this process at the remaining corners. With the tapping block and hammer, tap the spline down firmly and evenly all around. Trim any loose fibers at the joins with the knife. If any of the corners look less than perfect, trim them with your knife. Your job is complete.

Finishing Machine Cane

As with hand cane, it is not necessary to apply a finish to a machine-caned chair, but if a finish is desired, you can give your machine-caned chair the same treatment as a handwoven seat (see page 46).

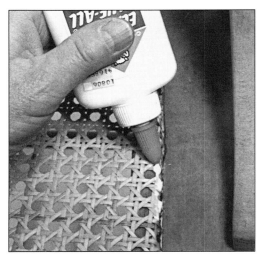

Run a glue bead approximately $1/8$ inch wide on the inside edge (cane side) of the groove.

Cut a 45-degree angle on the spline (see figure 2.8).

Tap the spline into a corner and tap it into the groove about halfway across the seat.

Mark the 45-degree angle for the next corner and undercut. Tap the spline firmly into place all the way across, using a block if necessary. Cut a new 45-degree angle on the end of the spline (not shown) to fit the corner just finished and fit it tightly into place. Repeat around the chair. Block the spline down with the square-edged wood block and hammer.

2.11 It will be easier to cut the spline if you use a back-and-forth rocking motion.

2.12 To add the next piece of spline, cut a 45-degree angle in the opposite direction and fit this to the corner just completed.

Some corners may not be perfect where the 45-degree angles meet.

Trim the corners neatly with a knife.

❖ Spline can be cut and joined on the middle of the side rails with the same 45-degree join. You may be forced to use short lengths of spline to complete a job, or a spline may split while curving around a tight corner. The splice should be centered near the middle of the side rails, not on the radius. A joint there will not fit snugly and will look untidy.

VARIATIONS
A barrel chair with concave shapes and deep curves

While machine cane is usually used in a flat plane, its use can be extended to shallow curves of a seat with concave front and back rails and to the deep curve of the back of a barrel chair. I suggest that you cane a rectangular seat before working on this type of project.

A seat with concave front and back rails is worked in the same way as a rectangular seat, except that extra care is needed to keep the cane webbing from pulling out of the curves. Work the curved front and back edges first, tapping the cane down into the groove in the center area and working alternately to the corners. Do the side (or straight) rails last. Take care not to stretch the cane into the side grooves, because the cane may pull out of the curved sections.

With a deep curve such as on the back of a barrel chair, allow at least 2 to 3 inches of margin all around. Lay the chair on its back. Begin tapping the cane into the groove in the center of the back, top and bottom, working

❖ An aberration that elicits bad words from caners is the use of staples to hold cane in the bottom of the groove, a practice that is totally unnecessary. With a chisel, gingerly pry out the spline and lift the staples by prying on the inner edge of the groove. Use side-cutting pliers to finish pulling out the staples.

A reproduction French bergère with machine-caned panels.

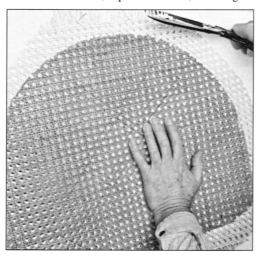

Use the old piece of cane from the chair as a pattern to cut out a new one, leaving a 1 to 2-inch margin all around. Cut the new cane dry, then soak it.

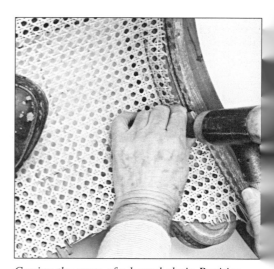

Caning the arms of a barrel chair. Position the cane so there is about one inch overlapping the groove all around. Lay the chair on the floor and use a foot if necessary to hold the cane in position.

gradually out to either side. To keep the cane from popping out, cut six 1-inch sections of oversize spline. Tap these temporary wedges lightly into the caned groove at the top and bottom of the back curve, spacing them about inches apart. Tap the cane into the grooves nd trim the surplus with scissors to a ³/₄- to 1-inch margin so that the cane bends down into the groove more easily. You may need to make relief cuts (figure 2.13) on the curves and the corners to coax the cane webbing into place. Keeping the chair on its back, trim the cane with the knife, glue and spline the curve, removing the temporary wedges.

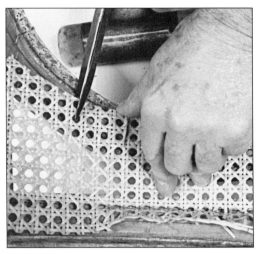

Make relief cuts on the curve to allow the cane to bend into the groove more easily.

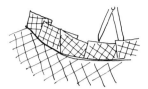

2.13 Relief cuts make possible the impossible.

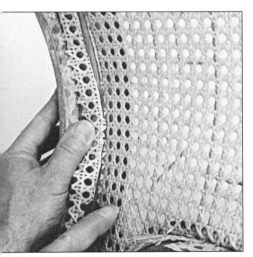

Caning the back of a barrel chair. Gently press the 1-inch surplus down with your thumb as you cut.

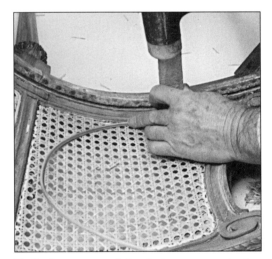

To fit the corners of the chair arm, start in the bottom corner and fit the spline all around the circumference without cutting it. The spline will need some coaxing into the tight radii of the other three "corners". Be sure your spline is very damp so that it will bend easily.

❖ Never precut spline; it never fits. On a circular seat make a 45-degree undercut to start, tap this end down in the center back area, and continue around until the spline overlaps the cut. Mark the spline, slide the wedge under it, and undercut with a 45-degree angle. Use care in making this last cut. If the spline is too long, it can be trimmed; if your cut is too short, you'll need to start over.

Suspended medallion

In the rare case of a suspended medallion in machine cane, install the full cane panel first. Lay the work flat on a table. Slide the medallion under the cane to the correct position. With scissors, cut out the shape of the medallion ³/₄ inch smaller than the shape formed by the groove (figure 2.14). Snip relief cuts every 2 inches, or as needed, but only as far as the inner edge of the groove. Lightly tap the cane into the groove of the medallion at top and bottom. Since this fixes the medallion's position, use great care to get it straight. The verticals in the cane can be used as guides. Tap the cane into the sides, then trim the cane just below the inner edge of the groove, using a freshly sharpened, razor-sharp knife. Glue and spline to complete. This whole operation has to be done straight through without pause, before the cane dries. After you're finished is the time for a good cup of coffee or tea.

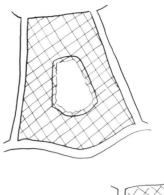

2.14 Cut out the shape of the medallion ³/₄ inch smaller than that formed by the groove.

OTHER MATERIALS
Radio Net and Swedish Modern

Radio Net and Swedish Modern cane webbing consist of horizontals and verticals alone, without diagonals. Both materials tend to get out of shape during installation and thus require special handling. Usually they are applied to a rectangular frame, chair back, cabinet door, or speaker front. They are not strong or durable enough to use in a chair seat.

Cut the cane 1 inch beyond the groove as usual. Position the damp cane over the frame and ravel the canes, one at a time, on all four sides until the woven cane fits exactly from the inner edge of the left groove to the inner edge of the right groove, and the same at top and bottom. Holding the cane on the frame in the correct position, push the ends down into the groove by hand with the maple wedge. The ends will bend easily with the cross strands removed. To trim, bend the ends

down flat on the frame with your thumb, holding six or eight ends down (figure 2.15). With the knife, cut just below the outside edge of the groove. Move to the next six ends and cut them. This prevents the ends from moving out of alignment when cut and/or pulling out of the groove. Install spline in the usual way.

To install Radio Net or Swedish Modern cane on a chair back with slanted posts, narrower at the bottom than at the top, ravel and anchor the top and bottom of the cane first, keeping the weave pattern straight. The sides, not raveled, are now trimmed with scissors to ³/₄ to 1 inch beyond the groove, no more. Snip relief cuts along the sides no deeper than the outside edge of the groove. Tap the cane into the groove either from the top down or the bottom up, alternating sides as you go to avoid distorting the cane. If this is not done carefully, the webbing will show a series of S curves.

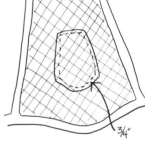

2.15 Installing Radio Net webbing. Ravel the ends and gently press them into the grooves. Bend the ends down flat on the frame with your thumb and cut just below the outside edge of the groove.

Giant Cane

Giant Cane, 1-inch mesh, is tough to handle. Soak it for 1 hour. The groove should be ¼ inch wide or a bit more, so that the large strands can be bent down in it.

Paper Cane

Paper Cane is found on chair backs, folding screens, and on inexpensive furniture. Usually it is installed with spline, the same as machine cane. Because it is a paper product, it disintegrates if it becomes too wet. Barely dampen it before installation. Because paper cane comes in large sizes, it works well for decorative projects such as wall screens. It isn't suitable for seats.

CORRECTING PAST SINS

A sad case is the fine walnut chair that was drilled for hand cane, but was later modified to accept machine cane by chiseling a groove. This treatment weakens the wooden frame considerably, sometimes disastrously. Ordinarily you'd need to repeat the crime with a machine cane replacement, but some chairs can be restored. Remove the old cane and spline. Disassemble the chair and glue a new, close-fitting spline into the groove, shaving it off flush with the wood frame. Redrill the holes from the bottom. The filler spline will be almost concealed when the binding goes on. While chiseling a groove over the holes is a form of wood butchery that will reduce the value of the piece considerably, it is still done, and unwitting customers pay for this mayhem.

ON GLUE

Putting large quantities of glue in the groove is a cardinal sin. It will splatter everywhere when you block down the spline, and it will make the spline very difficult to remove without grave damage to the frame, should the job come back for replacement. The inside glue bead, combined with the proper size spline, provides more than sufficient strength to hold the cane permanently. For a spline that refuses to stay in the groove in places where the groove may be slightly wider than in other areas, place a small block of wood over the spline and clamp it with a C-clamp until the glue is dry (figure 2.16).

Grooves that vary in width can be built up by cutting strips of veneer (¹/₂₈ inch thick) the depth of the groove. Glue them to the inner or outer vertical wall of the groove and clamp them by wedging a length of spline into the groove. This will help give the spline an even grip all the way around. Remove the temporary spline before installing the cane webbing.

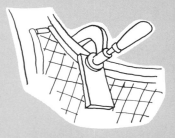

2.16 Where the groove is too wide, clamp the spline in place until the glue dries.

GALLERY

This graceful rocker dates from the 1880s or 1890s. It is American, made from hard maple, and grained to resemble rosewood. The maple, normally light in color, was stained a reddish-brown all over. Then black graining was applied by hand to the frontal or visible parts of the frame. This black dye does not yield to paint remover; most of it is indelible except where it has worn off on the arms and the seat front. The restoration and the hand caning are by the author.

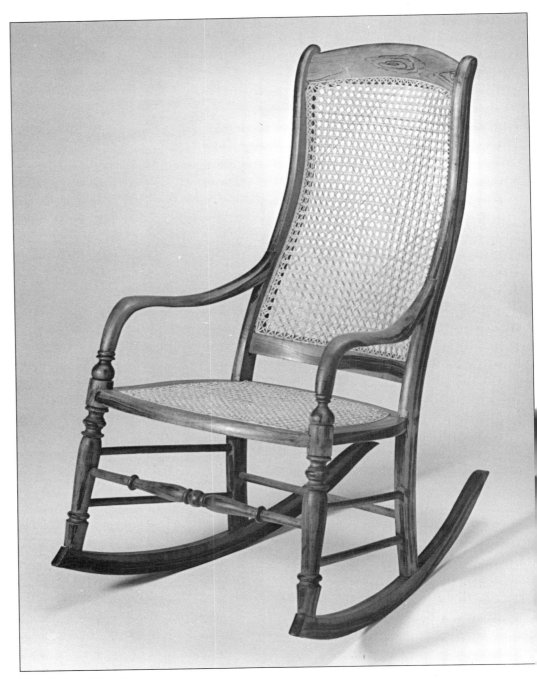

Photo: Gary Donnelly

Owners: Mr. and Mrs. Joel Bencan, Ambler, Pennsylvania

A reproduction, probably of Italian origin, this carved armchair has a hand-caned seat and back. The back has a suspended, carved, and pierced medallion supported by cane woven in a radial pattern. The cane in the back is pegged; the holes do not go through the frame.

Photo: Mark Archer

Owner: Iris M. Jack, Denver

Courtesy of Penthouse Refinishing Corporation

A carved reproduction of a French bergère, probably of Italian manufacture. It is contemporary, as shown by the use of machine cane in all panels; the chair was never drilled for hand cane but was grooved for spline from the beginning. The panels under the arms are double (cane is on both the inside and the outside of the arms). Fluted legs are characteristic of the Louis XVI style.

Photo: Mark Archer

Courtesy of Penthouse Furniture Refinishing Corporation, Denver

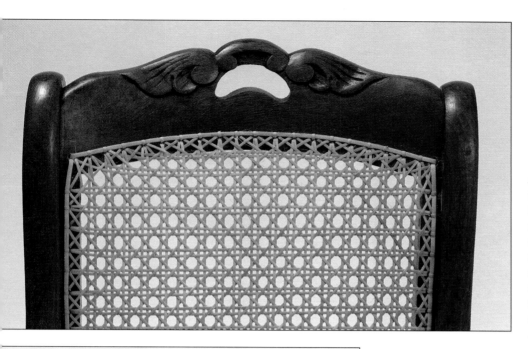

A child's walnut rocker with hand-caned seat and back is a handsome miniature of the more abundant, adult-size rockers of the time. Fewer children's chairs have survived. The saber legs at the front of the seat help to date this rocker from about 1840 to 1880.

Photo: Mark Archer
Courtesy of Wakely Furniture Shop, Aurora, Colorado

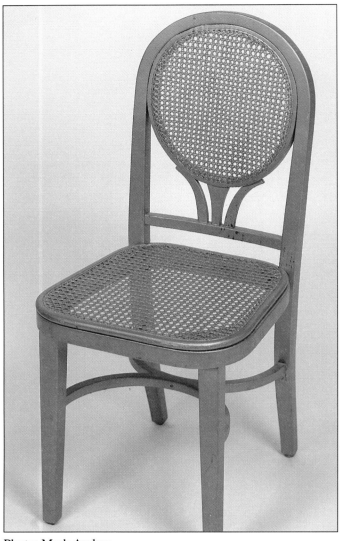

Photo: Mark Archer

Courtesy of Country Club Furniture Shop, Denver

Owner: Colorado Governor's Mansion (formerly the Boettcher Mansion), Denver

This gold-painted bentwood chair was made by Thonet of Vienna. It probably dates from the 1920s or 1930s. It is a ballroom chair which was used for social gatherings, and it might have been used by a small string orchestra at a musicale. The handwoven seat is a separate bentwood frame about ¹/₂ inch thick, nailed to the main frame; the Thonet company provided replacement seat frames with the cane woven in. The cane back may have been pegged from the front. Most Thonet chairs were grooved at the back of the holes; after caning, the groove was filled with a wooden spline finished level with the frame surface. This spline concealed the loops of cane on the back. Bentwood furniture spread worldwide before and after World War I; its style looks modern to this day.

Photo: Joe Coca

Owner: The author

From the 1890s, this maple chair has a round (but not quite, it's more of a subtle egg-shaped) seat. The squarish stance is characteristic of Eastlake style, as are the veined top slat and the beaded back posts. The small arms lend strength at a weak point. You had better be very skillful with a bandsaw (and your hands) if you wish to reproduce one of these arms from scratch.

Heavily used by firemen in their off-duty moments, this is a firehouse Windsor from the 1890s, with maple for the stretchers, legs, and spindles, and oak for the steam-bent parts. This chair is also called a schoolteacher's chair. For use as a desk chair, the lower part often has a swivel-and-tilt mechanism on casters in place of the legs. In many cases, the cane back is much taller than this example. The cane size is superfine.

This back view of the firehouse Windsor shows off the rich detail of a hand-caned job.

Photo: Joe Coca
Owner: The author

This steel tubing chair of the 1960s with a natural rush seat is a thinner cousin to the Italian Chiavari chairs made of beechwood belonging to that period. They have two to five slats in the back and a rush-type seat made of various materials such as sea grass, plain grass, or Danish rope.

Photo: Joe Coca

Owner: The author

A detail of an ash mule-ear chair, contemporary. The lovely pale green color of this newly rushed chair will soon fade to a warm golden brown like the rush chair on the next page.

Below, the gilt decoration on the top slat is my attempt at gold leafing. It is in the style of "fancy chairs" of the 1840s.

Photo: Joe Coca
Owner: The author

On this "fancy chair" of 1830 to 1850, the gold-leaf distelfink (Pennsylvania Dutch for "thistle finch") on the top slat and the natural rush seat are by the author. This chair is a cousin to the vast tribe of Hitchcock chairs manufactured at that time.

Inset: detail of the underside of the chair.

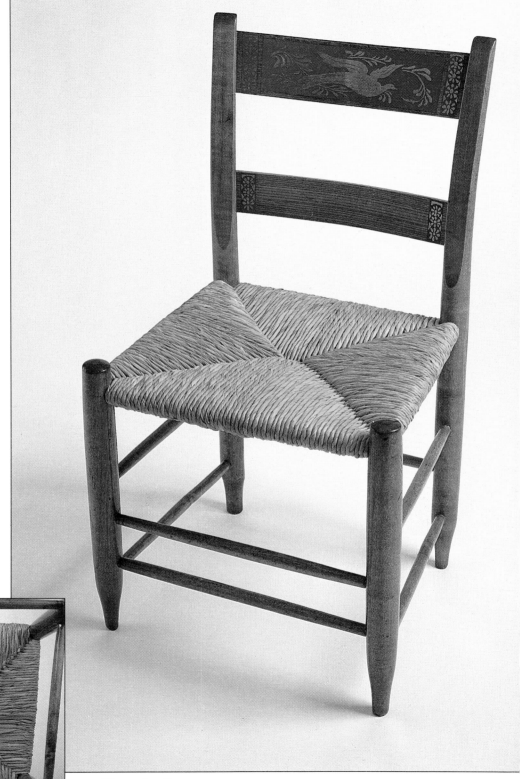

Photo: Joe Coca
Owner: Bertha Tschetter, Denver

An American primitive from New England, this slat-back rocker sports a very durable hickory splint seat. In time, this beautiful wood will burnish to a fine patina. It may take a hundred years, but that's how long this seat may last. The stubby, knife rockers are characteristic of Shaker work, but this is probably not an authentic Shaker chair.

Photo: Mark Archer

Owner: Doris Eggleston, Denver, Colorado

This walnut Eastlake-style rocker with matched veneer on the top slat is woven in 6 mm cane in the twill pattern. It dates from the 1880s or 1890s.

Photo: Joe Coca

Owner: Inez Gamble, Brighton, Colorado

RUSH

CHAPTER III

Imitation rush
> *step-by-step procedure*
> *other patterns*
> *other materials*

Natural rush
> *weaving the basic shape*
> *variations*
> *other materials and equipment*

Slat-back ladder-back chair with a trapezoidal seat woven in imitation rush. The step-by-step process for weaving this seat begins on the next page. Chair courtesy of the Woodshop, Carbondale, Colorado.

Rush, a world apart from cane, gets its name from bulrushes, the material which was traditionally used to weave this type of seat. Rush also refers to a wrapping technique in which a length of rush rope is wound in and out and around the rungs (rails) of a chair. Rushwork's age-old technique produces one pattern of four triangles which more or less meet in the center of the seat. Only slight variations are possible. Rush seats rate high in durability, and their firm surface is often eased with a cushion. Rush has been used traditionally on simple, utilitarian, rustic furniture, yet today it appears in decorator shops as high style, valued for its warm character.

Chairs suitable for rush have round rails, hand-hewn rails which may have flats on the outside, or flat rails mortised or doweled together with a recess cut for the rush. I recommend using either the traditional cattail or imitation rush. If rush is a new endeavor for you, you should start with imitation rush. It's readily available and easier to handle, as you don't have to make your own rope as you do with natural rush. When you have mastered it, try using the natural material.

IMITATION RUSH CHAIR

Our example is a slat-back ladder-back with a trapezoidal seat in which the front rail is longer than the back rail (figure 3.1). Shapes such as this with sloping side rails present the major problem in laying out rush.

After you have learned to deal with this type, you will be able to handle rectangular and square seats with ease; these simpler shapes are omitted here.

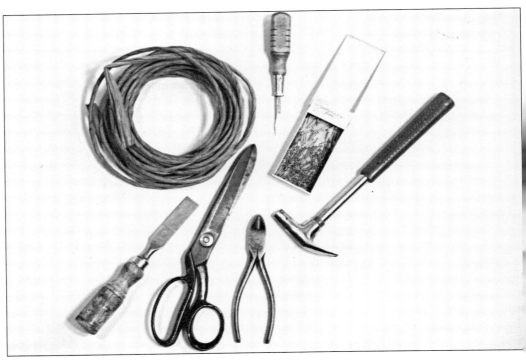

The primary tools for working with imitation rush: medium-sized "brown art fiber", stubby screwdriver, ¹/₂-inch flat-headed nails (not brads), small hammer, scissors, and side-cutting pliers. The ³/₄-inch chisel or the side-cutting pliers can be used singly or together for cutting off the old seat.

Materials and Tools

You'll need a hammer, 3/16-inch screwdriver, medium-sized side-cutting pliers, ruler or tape measure, corrugated cardboard for stuffing, pencil, and scissors (hefty upholsterer's scissors work best). You'll also need a bucket of water, some 18-gauge, 1/2-inch flat-headed nails, and a low table to place your chair on for working. You may also need a file or rasp to rough up the rungs if they are very smooth.

Use a medium-sized "brown art fiber" rush, 5/32 or 6/32 inch in diameter. This imitation rush is rope twisted from a 2-inch-wide strip of kraft paper. A 2-lb coil is enough for an average-sized seat; a 33-lb roll does 12 to 15 seats.

Larger and smaller imitation rush is available, but its use is usually limited to matching an existing chair in a set. The smaller the rush, the more time consuming and tedious it will be to weave; the larger the rush, the bulkier the final appearance of the seat. Since the size of the rush used does not affect the strength of the seat, any size can be used. Decisions will be based largely on your aesthetic sense.

"Green variegated" rush is randomly dyed brown art fiber. It is made to imitate the look of natural rush; you must decide if it succeeds. The rush that I prefer is made by Sackner, in North Carolina, and it is available through a number of retail outlets (see Suppliers). I find that other manufacturers either twist the rope rock-hard or use recycled paper that disintegrates when damp.

Preparation

Assemble your materials. Cut off a length of imitation rush about 10 yards long, enough to make a hand-sized coil 6 to 8 inches in diameter and 1 inch thick. Give a good bend and pinch to the end on the roll and to the end in your hand so that they will be easy to find. Soak this working coil 10 to 15 minutes to soften it. Remove it from the water, and add another coil to the water, and so on until the chair is done. Weaving with dry rope is an exercise in frustration. It will cause gaps in the weaving, a sure sign of a rank amateur.

While your rope is soaking, remove the old rush; heavy side-cutting pliers or lever-aged tin snips with serrated blades work best. Cut about an inch inside the rails all around, bending the cut rush ends down off the rails. Pull out the tacks with pliers. Push the whole seat downward to remove it. If the rails have sharp edges, round them with a file. Sloping side rails, especially if they go in steeply toward the back, should be roughed with a rasp and/or notched shallowly on the outer edges to hold the rush in place.

Place the chair facing you on a low, sturdy, 18- to 22-inch-high table so that you can stand and work from the front. Measure the distance between the back posts. Center this measurement on the front rail, marking each end with a pencil. This represents an imaginary rectangle for the rush pattern. The triangles which will be worked between the front legs and the pencil marks are called "gussets" (figure 3.1). It is necessary to weave these gussets to fill in the front corners before the rest of the front rail can be woven. If the gussets are not woven first, the back will fill in before the front, leaving a gap unwoven on the front rail with no way to complete it.

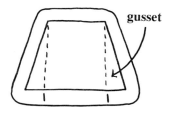

3.1 The gussets on a trapezoidal seat need to be woven before starting the center rectangle.

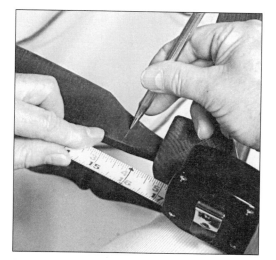

Mark the width of the distance between the back posts onto the front rail, centered.

Weaving the Gussets

To begin the gusset, nail the end of the rush one-third of the way back from the front on the inner edge of the left rail. Start the nail in the rope as you hold it on top of the rail (figure 3.2). Turn the rope to the inside and nail it securely. I don't find staples acceptable because they pull out when the cord is tensioned; carpet tacks are too thick for this job, and may split the wood.

Bring the hand coil of rush over the left end of the front rail. With your left thumb, hold the rush in place on the front rail—*never* release tension on the rope you are weaving with. With your right hand, bring the coil up through the center of the seat and drop it over the left rail. Pull the weaver tight as it goes over and around the front rail, comes up through the seat, and crosses itself as it goes over the left rail. Make this right-angle turn tight against the post with minimal gap. There is no need whatever to stick a pencil in this gap to make the turn more of a right angle, as some books suggest. Tighten the rope on the left rail, and hold it with your thumb and forefinger. With your other hand, take the coil up through the center and over the right rail. Pull it tight and hold it. Bring the coil up through the center again and over the front rail. Pull tight and hold. Pull the cord to a point one-third back from the front on the right rail and nail it as you did the other end (figure 3.3). Cut the rope and start again on the left rail, nailing the end directly behind the first one. These individual pieces of rope will fill the gussets, so that you will have an empty

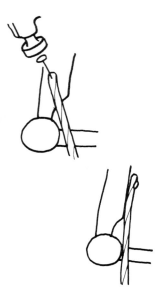

3.2 Start the nail in the rope on the top of the rail, then nail it securely to the inside.

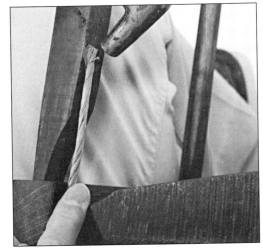

Tack the starting rope on the inner face of the left rail.

3.3 Finish by nailing the rope securely to the right rail. Cut off the end.

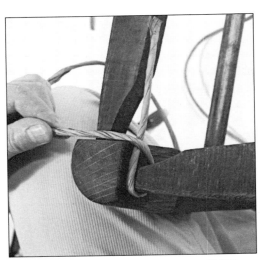

To weave the gussets, bring the rope OVER the front rail, then UNDER, then make a right-angle turn to the left. Pull tight. Do not let go of the rope. Bring the rope over the left rail, then under it and to the center of the seat.

Cross over to the right front rail and go OVER the right rail, UNDER it, up through the center area of the seat, and make a right turn, then go OVER the front rail. Bring the rope under the front rail and nail it to the right seat rail.

rectanglar area to work for the main body of the seat. Repeat this operation until the front rail is covered up to the pencil marks. Straighten the loops on each rail by crowding them together (figure 3.4). Because the rope is damp, it is malleable and will pack together nicely. You may need to add another length of rope to fill out to the pencil mark. Measure to be sure that the distance between the back posts is equal to the distance between the wraps of rush on the front.

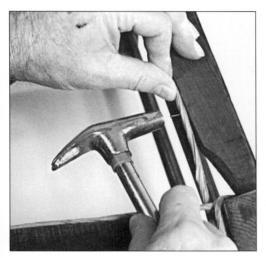

Nail the rope to the inside of the right seat rail to correspond with the other end of it. Cut off the rope ¹/₂ inch beyond the nail.

Repeat this procedure until the strands reach the pencil marks.

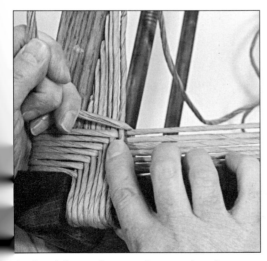

At the right-angle turns, be sure that the two ropes already woven (the horizontal one below and the vertical one on top) are pinched tightly together when the rope you are working with makes the next right turn.

Check the strands often to be sure that they are straight from front to back and from right to left. Crowd the rope back with the hammer.

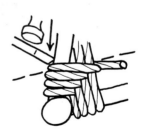

3.4 Use a screwdriver and hammer to crowd the ropes up against the rail. The two sides should line up with each other.

ALTERNATE METHODS FOR FILLING THE GUSSETS OR "GAINING" ON THE FRONT RAIL

An alternate method for filling in the gussets can be done without nails as follows: cut three lengths of rush each 8 feet long, fold them in half and tie the loop thus made with a generous length of stout twine. Tie the twine on the back rail at the left so that the rope loop is about 3 or 4 inches from the back rail. Weave the cut ends one at a time around the two front posts (figure 3.6). Take their tails around the back rail and anchor them with a clothespin. When three rush lengths have been woven in this way, tie them together with twine and tie the twine on the back rail. Trim the rush ends. Additional rush loops may be needed to fill out to the pencil marks. This method invites a loss of tension that does not serve our purpose well. It could be used on a frame of steel tubing.

Another method for "gaining" on the front rail, is by weaving additional rounds around the front posts. Tie or nail the starting end to the left rail. Take the rush around all four posts, weaving around twice on the front posts, left and right (figure 3.7). Make complete rounds, doubling every other one on the front rail. Frequently measure the spaces at the back rail and at the front rail until they become equal. There is no need to mark the front rail with this method because establishing the perfect rectangle will happen farther in on the front rail than the pencil marks of the conventional method. After the spaces on the front and back rails have become equal, proceed as for our ladder-back chair example with one continuous strand of rope. This method may be faster than the regular method as a full, fat coil of rush is used and there's no delay for nailing. However, the finished appearance is not as neat because the second turns around the posts aren't as crisp, leaving the corners more rounded.

❖ Ordinarily, a rush seat is completed in a day. With experience and improved efficiency, two can be done. That's a heavy order. Incomplete work can be left overnight or for a week. To hold the tension during the first two-thirds of the weaving, pull a loop from the weaving rope down between two center ropes, those that will be buried. As the seat closes up, you can hook a loop through the weaving area to accomplish the same thing.

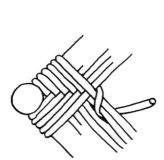

3.5 "Parking" the weaver.

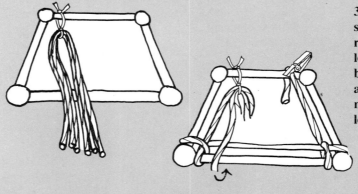

3.6 Instead of nailing short lengths along the rail to weave the gussets, long lengths of rope may be tied on the back rail and woven in the same manner as the short lengths.

3.7 Additional rounds may be woven around the front posts to gain on the front rail.

Filling In the Center Of the Seat

With the gussets filled in, you are ready to weave the center of the seat with a continuous piece of rush. Nail the starting end on the left rail and wrap it as you did for the short pieces. Instead of nailing it to the right post after you've wrapped the front right post, continue over the back rail. Bring the coil up in the center, over the right rail, up in the center, over the left rail, and so on around and around the chair. There is a rhythm to this wrapping which will become second nature, and there should be no question of where you need to go next.

It is a bad idea to try to wrap two corners by placing the rope around loosely and then tightening it. Tension is lost, and it will show in the finished job. Dragging the working coil along is unavoidable; at least it does get smaller. Time can be saved by using a relatively larger coil in the beginning. You will need six or more coils to complete the seat; as the center hole closes up, use a smaller coil, and at the last only a single strand that can be pulled through the center hole.

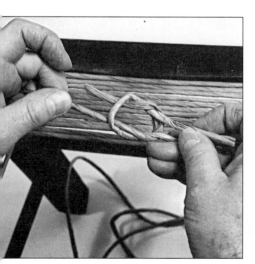

When you add a new coil, join the ends with a square knot, positioning the knot in the center part of the seat. As the weaving closes up, the knots will be located on the underside of the seat and will be tucked under adjacent strands at the finish of the weaving.

Try to keep your working coil intact as long as possible. It will probably get tangled eventually, and then it just has to be sorted out. An alternative to handling the coil is wrapping the rush around a shuttle of cardboard or thin wood, but I find that the shuttle is more a hindrance than a help. You will have to give it up anyway when the center of the seat closes. Another alternative is to place the coil in a plastic bag which will keep it damp and minimize fraying, but this, too, imposes an unnecessary struggle. Long experience has shown that weaving the rush bare is the best method to finish the job expeditiously.

When beginning a new coil, join the ends with a square knot (figure 3.8). During, and up to, the first two-thirds of weaving, tie the knots in the central area on any of the four sides, away from the right-angle turns where the rush crosses itself. In these four triangular areas (figure 3.9), the strands will be sandwiched between the top and bottom layers of the seat. During the last third of weaving, you won't have access to these strands, so tie the knots on the underside 1 inch in from the rail on any of the four sides. Avoid knots on the rail or close to the right-angle turns. Of course, none should be topside.

After six or seven rounds, check that the loops over the rails are straight. They must line up parallel left to right and front to back. This constant checking every half dozen strands is imperative; otherwise the center area will be a disaster. Pound the offenders back with a hammer and screwdriver (figure 3.10). Judge the alignment by eye. Either lay a straight edge across the seat or step to the side and sight across. It pays to check the back of the back rung to see if the rush runs vertically over it. Pound the lower part of the loop back to straighten it if needed (figure 3.11). This area needs your frequent attention because it is out of your sight most of the time. In rushwork, a sense of touch is our most valuable tool. By touch, be sure that the rope does not double up on top of the previ-

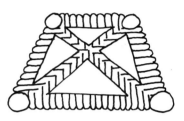

3.8 A square knot.

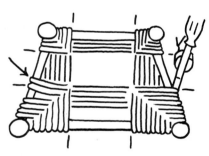

3.9 Tie knots in the triangular areas.

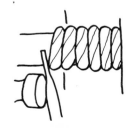

3.10 Pound the weavers into place with a hammer and a screwdriver.

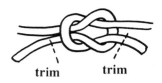

3.11 If necessary, pound the lower part of the loop.

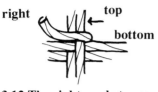

3.12 The right-angle turns should be tight but should not crowd the previous cross strands.

ous one as it goes around the rung. This may happen if the rush has crept out of alignment.

The right-angle turns merit special attention. As the weaving rope comes up through the center area, be sure to push the bottom cross strand upward, forcing the two strands together. The steps in this movement are as follows: push the bottom cross strand toward the center of the seat, pull the weaver up

tight, make the turn, and push the top cross strand downward, tightening the weaver across it, being sure it does not override the previous cross strand (figure 3.12). If the cross strands are allowed to slip back on their neighbors, the right-angle turn will not be sharp, and the strands will not be parallel to each other. The corners will collapse, and weaving the center will be impossible.

Adding the Stuffing

After completing about one-third of the weaving, insert corrugated cardboard stuffing that you have cut to fit the four sides (slopping the triangle to fit the slope of the side rails—figure 3.13), each layer smaller than the last to form a stairstep edge at the center (figure 3.14). Clean cardboard cartons are free at the grocer's or other stores. Three layers of cardboard triangles should be enough to fill the space flush with the top of the rung (figure 3.15). The cardboard points fit into

pockets made by the rush. Cut the tips off the front and back cardboard triangles to leave a 1- to 1¼-inch gap in the center through which you will weave; you'll have to bring the coil of rush up through this space.

You can use other materials for stuffing, such as crumpled kraft paper or newspapers (it's interesting to find a newspaper from 1932 in an old seat), but I strongly prefer cardboard because it is neater, stronger, and smoother.

3.13 Cut the cardboard to fit the sloping sides of the chair.

Cut four cardboard triangles so that they fit the sloping sides of the chair (figure 3.13). Tuck the corners of the triangles into the top pockets.

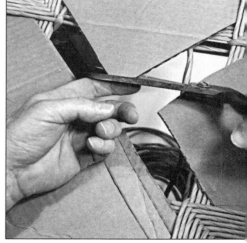

Trim off the points of the cardboard to leave extra space in the center (about 1¼ inches wide). The coil will move through this space as you wrap.

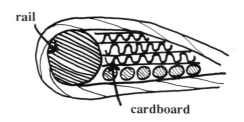

rail

cardboard

.14 For this chair, three layers of cardboard are ufficient. The rule of thumb is to fill in the height f the rail with stuffing. The cardboard is airstepped so that the rush will curve gradually own to the center.

3.15 Sideview of cardboard stuffing.

Closing Up the Center

After the left and right sides of the seat are ull, close the center gap with a continuous figure eight. At this stage, you'll have to work vith a single strand because the space is so mall. After weaving three or four rounds, ound them close together with the screwriver and hammer (figure 3.16). Check the traightness of the ropes, front to back. Enarge the center space with the screwdriver or the last two strands. When the rope begins

to untwist so it is hard to force through the small hole, cut the weaving end of the rope back several inches, to make a fresh end. Nail the last rope on the bottom of the back rail and cut it, leaving a 3-inch tail. Use the screwdriver to help you tuck the tail under the neighboring strands. Tuck exposed knots between and under adjacent strands. Smooth out the top of the seat by lightly pounding it with the side of the hammer.

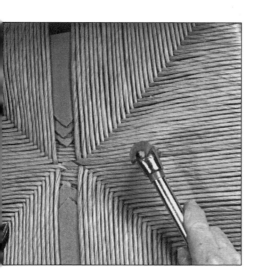

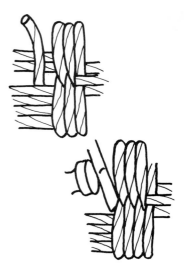

After completely filling the sides, smooth out the last strands by lightly pounding with a hammer. Close up the center by wrapping figure eights back and forth. When starting the figure eights, push a loop of the rope through the center and then pull the rest of the rope through.

3.16 Close up the center by weaving figure eights. After several rows, pound the rounds close together.

The finished chair.

Finishing

Because it is a paper product, imitation rush will soak up anything in sight and must be sealed. The best finish is three coats of 3-lb-cut white shellac. Allow four hours' drying time between coats. Certain brands of imitation rush show a "raised grain" reaction after the first coat. When the first coat is completely dry, steel wool the fuzzies and apply two more coats of shellac. After all of the shellac coats have dried, you may add several coats of polyurethane varnish. This finish gives a plastic-coated, glassy appearance which may or may not be to your taste. Normally rush is not colored or stained, as the shellac darkens it slightly.

A "pickled" finish can be made by sealing the rush with one coat of shellac and then giving it a turpentine wash with a white or colored oil paint mixed in. The wash should be very thin: about 1 oz of turpentine mixed with a 1-inch squirt of paint is enough for one chair seat. After coating with the turpentine wash, lightly brush the tops of the strands with a rag for an "antique" look. When dry, apply two coats of shellac. By this means, you can match an original color.

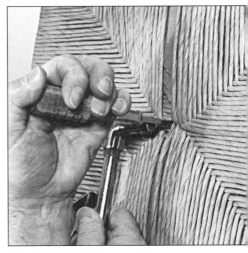

Use the screwdriver and hammer to crowd the strands together and help open a space to weave through. At the last, wiggle the screwdriver to enlarge the opening so that you can pull through the weaving end.

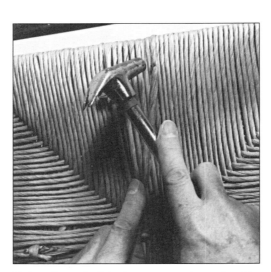

Bring the end of the last rope to the underside and nail it to the bottom of the rail.

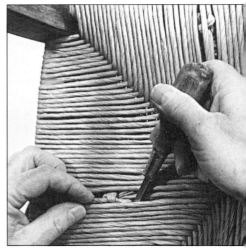

Cut the end off, leaving a 3-inch tail. Tuck it in and tuck the knots under adjacent strands on the underside. Seal your new seat with shellac or another finish.

OTHER PATTERNS
Round Seats

The basic technique described above is used for all other imitation rush jobs. Even a round seat can be rushed. It may have exposed raised blocks at the four "corners", or they may be wrapped with rope with the regular pattern woven over it (figure 3.17). Weaving a round shape is very much like weaving a square. There are no gussets to fill, and there will be no figure eights to weave in the center. On the steep curve (about the 2, 4, 8 and 10 o'clock positions), it may be necessary to untwist the rope slightly to make it thicker as it goes around the rail front in order to "gain", and so that the pattern stays parallel.

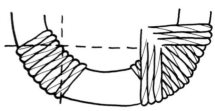

3.17 On a round seat, wrap the corners with rope to mark them, then weave as usual.

Chair Backs

On a rocker back on which both sides are public, knots on the buried strands are acceptable because they won't be seen. However to avoid knots on the outside, begin each new strand by nailing the cord with a square butt joint on the back of the rail (figure 3.18). One layer of cardboard stuffing on each side, front and back, should be sufficient. Special care and experience must be called into action to make the back almost as neat as the front.

3.18 To avoid knots on the outside of a seat back, butt join the ends on the back of the rail. Secure the ends with nails.

Slip Seats

In the case of a slip seat (a separate frame that sits down into, or on top of, another frame) with rush covering the corners, the rush pattern is "half-woven" to cover the wood all the way to the inner corner of the frame (figure 3.19). Pound down the nailed ends well so that there will be a minimal bump when the regular rush covers them. Treat all four corners alike, with the final cords pointing as shown (figure 3.20). Measure the distance between the back corners (or between the woven rush) and mark it on the front rail, then fill in the gusset as described for the ladder-back chair. When about six rounds are complete, pound down the corner areas so they lie flat. The remainder of the weaving is done as usual.

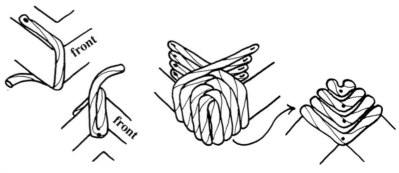

3.19 Covering the corners on a slip seat.

3.20 After the corners have been worked, weave the gussets as usual.

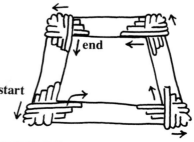

A square stool with an imitation rush seat. Courtesy of Verna J. Hames.

Decorative Seats

For a more decorative seat, you can double and triple the strands left to right. This has the effect of pushing the crossing in the center for the figure eights farther back in the seat. Nail the beginning rope on and weave the gusset on the left as usual. Then weave a figure eight between the right and left side rails before wrapping the right front corner as usual. Continue to fill the gusset to the pencil marks

3.21 Weave figure eights from side to side to move the center crossing farther back on the chair seat.

with single strands, alternating figure eights with normal wraps (figure 3.21). Usually the last half-dozen rounds are woven in the regular manner (without doubling) into the center (figure 3.22) until the central area of figure eights begins. This pattern is weaker than plain, ordinary rushing, in which each rope is firmly anchored.

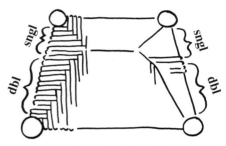

3.22 By weaving additional figure eights left and right, you can change the position of the center crossing point. Here, the rush has been doubled on the left and right rails, lengthening the central quadrant and shortening the back.

Other Variations

Other complications confront people who work in rush. Among them is the Hitchcock chair with wood battens on the sides and back and half-round trim at the front. These trim pieces must be carefully removed before weaving the rush, and reaffixed when the rush is complete. Some Windsor chairs have rush that goes through a crack at the back. This space is made by an additional rail

fastened with countersunk screws. Dig out the wood plugs with a narrow chisel, remove the screws, and move the rail backward at least an inch to give yourself some weaving space. On some styles, the back rail and spindles must be removed entirely. Cast a wary eye on Hitchcocks and Windsors; they demand much more work than just the rushing.

OTHER MATERIALS

Danish rope sometimes appears in the rush pattern. Woven dry, Danish rope needs extreme tension to make square turns and halfway neat figure eights. I haven't found this material well suited for this application. Seagrass has the same disadvantage. Valued for its texture, it is best in some type of basketweave. Macramé rope made of either

hemp or synthetic material is a possibility, though its durability is questionable. Nylon rope is beastly: it's too slick to keep in place, and it sags considerably under a warm behind. Polypropylene rope, cotton braided clothesline, and plastic-covered clothesline have been, and are, used, but none offers serious competition to the traditional materials.

NATURAL RUSH

Although natural rush is laid out and woven exactly the same as imitation rush is, greater skill is required to handle it because you need to make rope as you work. Experience in weaving imitation rush is an absolute prerequisite.

The raw material used in this country is the leaves of cattails (*Typha latifolia*), which commonly grow wild in swampy areas. English rush weavers use what is considered to be the true bulrush *Scirpus lacustris*; here I refer to cattails as rushes.

You must harvest and cure the rush yourself. In Colorado, cattails are ready for cutting in late August when the tips have turned brown. Find an area with few seed heads and cut only those plants without them. Use heavy scissors or hand pruners to cut the stalks about a foot above the ground or water. Waterproof boots or waders are helpful in shallow ponds, but most rush is accessible from dry ground. Standing on the cut stumps will keep you from sinking in muck, for a while.

Rush cutting offers fringe benefits: you may have an audience of ducks and geese asking questions. A few stalks with seed heads will make a fine bouquet. Dry the stalks flat on a table for a week, then spray the heads with Krylon to keep the fuzz from flying. Arranged in a pot, they make a pleasant sight for winter days.

As you cut the stalks, lay them on the bank, butts together. Discard short and broken pieces. Do not break the leaves, as the broken ones will snap when they are woven.

A natural rush chair of contemporary American origin. The decorated top slat is my attempt at gold leaf.

❖ Native Americans made flour from the brown, velvety cattail seed head, ate the roots, and used the leaves for floor covering and baskets. A useful plant, indeed, besides furnishing seating material.

Spread the rushes out and dry them for a week, turning them over every day. Don't pile them too thickly or they will mildew. Mine dry quite well spread on a concrete walk in the autumn sun. More color will be retained if the rushes are dried on a shaded porch. The soft greens in a freshly woven seat are beautiful to behold, though the chlorophyll will depart in a year or two, fading to tan and gold. Be sure your customers understand this course of events before you start working on their chairs to avoid their dismayed comment, "But the new seat does not match others in my set!"

When the cattails are crisp, tie the rushes in 6-inch bundles, butts at one end, and store in a dry place, such as a loft or garage. Handle them like eggs: don't step on, run over, or crush them. Properly prepared cattails will keep for years. You will find dried rushes shrunken considerably from the quantity you picked. Make note of this for the next cutting. Remember that dryness is essential to storing cattails; otherwise, you will have a giant crop of black mildew. Rushes are available in the wild only about one month of the year. If you don't have access to cattails, you can purchase them (see Suppliers), but be prepared for heavy damage in shipping as they are delicate.

The use of this natural, renewable resource with its subtle coloring of sage green, gold, and tan is a great satisfaction to the maker, observer, and sitter. I think you'll find, as I have, that the warmth and earthiness of a natural rush chair seat is irresistible.

❖ Uniform rope size depends on your sense of touch. A first attempt with rush is apt to be less than perfect, but the next job will improve 100 percent. Because of the irregular nature of this natural material, minor variations in rope size and texture are unavoidable, yet practice brings excellent results. For your first natural rush job, I suggest that you try a chair or stool seat that requires medium to large rope.

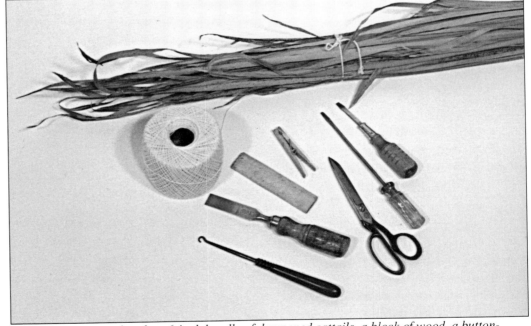

Materials for natural rush: a 6-inch bundle of dampened cattails, a block of wood, a button-hook or homemade wire hook, scissors, screwdriver, ³/₄-inch chisel, spring-type wooden clothes-pin, heavy-duty string, and a 10-inch-high stool.

Tools

Tools consist of scissors, an old-fashioned buttonhook or a substitute made from a coat hanger, and a small clothes wringer, the kind that fastened onto the side of a washtub. This last item is essential but may be difficult to find. Enlist the help of antique dealers. Secondhand and thrift shops and garage sales are good places to look. Other incidentals for rushing are a spring-type wooden clothespin, a 9-by-12-foot plastic drop cloth, and string such as medium-sized crochet thread, waxed linen shoemaker's thread, or heavy carpet warp. Finally, you'll need a ³/₄-inch chisel to remove the old chair seat.

There are slightly different approaches to making a rush seat. I evolved these methods over hundreds of rush seats and many years of experience.

Preparing the Rush

The day before weaving the seat, dampen the rushes. Spread the plastic drop cloth, doubled to 4¹/₂ by 12 feet, on a concrete or waterproof floor. Lay the rushes in the center, butts together. (About two 6-inch bundles will be enough for one seat.) Spray the top of the pile with a bathroom disinfectant to discourage mildew. Any brand will do, provided the label mentions mildew. Sprinkle the rushes with about two gallons of lukewarm water. Fold over the sides and then the ends of the drop cloth. After several hours or before retiring, roll the bundle over on its top to let the water dribble through to the top rushes, and leave overnight. Twelve hours is about the minimum dampening time; 24 is more than enough. Dampening can't be hurried, and crispy rush is impossible to use. In cool weather, if the rush is outdoors, and the temperature is between 35° and 50° F, the dampened rush will keep for three days at the most. At temperatures above 60° F, it will begin to rot after two days. This time frame dictates completing the seat in one sitting or at most, in one and a half days.

Getting Ready To Weave

The most effective method I've found for cutting off the old seat is to slide a ³/₄-inch chisel flat along the rail tops. Turn the chair as you work, cutting toward the corner posts for optimum leverage. Unhook the edges of the rush and push the seat downward. As this is a dirty job, I suggest that you work outdoors. Clean the dirt off the rungs with a rag or vacuum. Check for hundred-dollar bills inside the old seat before discarding it.

Pull out a 2-inch-diameter bunch from the wet rushes, holding the butt ends. Rewrap those remaining. Run this bunch through the wringer twice, butt ends first, to remove surplus water and air. They will crack like firecrackers. Lay the bunch on the floor near you, butt ends within easy reach. I prefer sitting on a 10-inch-high stool on a smooth, rugless floor and holding the chair clamped between my knees. This allows me to rotate the chair with ease and provide the necessary bracing.

❖ *Alternative method of crushing the leaves.* If you can't find a clothes wringer, you can accomplish the same task by hand, though much more slowly. Pull each rush, tip first, over the back of a kitchen knife, holding a thumb on the rush leaf. This crushes out the air and removes extra water. Perhaps you can enlist an apprentice rusher with very durable thumbs for this job.

Take a 2-inch bundle of cattails (rushes) and run them through a clothes wringer twice.

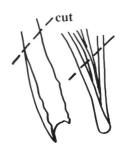

3.23 Cut off the thick ends, or boles, of the rushes at an angle.

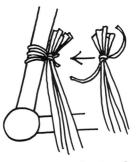

3.24 Tie the butt ends of eight or ten rushes together with string. Then tie this bundle to the inside of the left rail, halfway back.

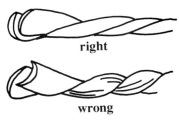

right

wrong

3.25 The leaves have a natural curve. Nest them together so that the curves are all in the same direction.

In commercial operations, a rotating table with the chair clamped to it is used. Such a tool is worth making if you are faced with a set of 12 chairs, but for a small number it isn't necessary.

As with our imitation rush chair, this seat is a standard ladder-back with sloping side rails. Begin as you did with the imitation rush chair by measuring the back rail, and center-ing and marking this distance on the front rail to make a perfect rectangle (see page 75).

With scissors, cut the thick ends off the rushes so that the leaves fall free (figure 3.23). Use an angling cut. Place trimmings aside to use as stuffing. Use this prepared rush immediately. It will stay workable for about an hour, depending on the temperature and breezes.

Weaving the Gussets

With an 18-inch-long piece of string, tie the butt ends of eight or ten rushes tightly to-gether and then tie the bunch to the inside left rail, halfway back (figure 3.24). Select three or four leaves from the bunch. You'll notice that the leaves have a natural curve. Arrange the "cup" of leaves together like nesting spoons and twist this cup inward (figure 3.25) *away* from the left front post (figure 3.26). Determine the diameter of the twist at this point; few or smaller leaves will make a thin-ner rope, larger or more leaves, a fatter one. I find that one large and two small leaves or two large ones do the trick. Make a long, smooth twist rather than a short, bumpy one

(figure 3.27). Practice twisting the rope tighter and looser until you have the feel of working with it. When you feel confident, begin working the gussets as you did for the imitation rush chair seat (page 76).

Probably the trickiest aspect of working with natural rush is coordinating the weaving and the twisting of rope. Like anything else, this will take some practice; I suggest that you practice awhile before you begin in ear-nest on your project.

To complicate things further, you'll need to reverse the direction of the twist twice as you go around the posts. Although you could twist the rope in the same direction for the

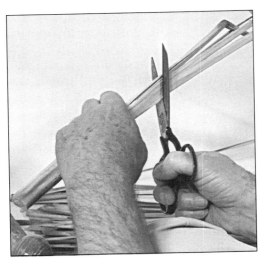

Cut off the thick ends of the rushes.

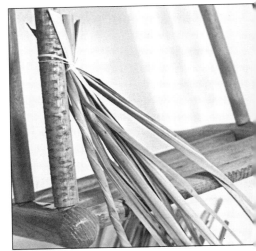

Tie a bundle of eight to ten rushes to the left side rail. Use three or four to start making rope, twisting away from the post.

duration of the weaving (after all, imitation rush is worked this way), not reversing the twist will cause new leaves added to the rope to pop out of place. (You'll understand this better as you begin working.)

Twisting the rope

Twisting works like this: As you approach the left front rail, twist the rope clockwise 2 to 3 inches beyond the rail. Go over and

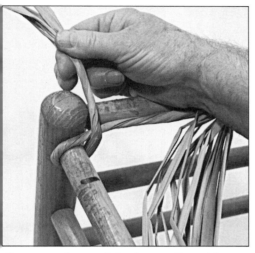

Go over and around the front rail, working the gussets as you did for the imitation rush chair seat.

Adding a new leaf to the rope.

around the front rail and reverse the twist at the point where you make the right-angle turn. You will now be twisting counterclockwise. Go over and around the left rail and reverse the direction of the twist again on the bottom side of the rail. You're now twisting clockwise (figure 3.28). Repeat in the same manner for the other side. Finish by temporarily clamping the ends with a clothespin to the back rail.

As you work, you'll notice that sometimes you'll need to use your right hand to make the twist and sometimes your left hand: coming over the front rail, use your right hand to make the twist; your left thumb and forefinger hold the twist in place and move up the cord. Don't let go. Bring the rush rope up the center. Now the left hand makes the twist, *away from the post* (figure 3.28). Always maintain tension on the rope, pulling the rope tight around the rail and snug against the post.

To keep the diameter of your rope consistent, take another rush from your pile (probably a small one), butt first, and add it to your rope while holding the two rushes in tension with the fingers of the right hand (figure 3.29). Give several sharp twists to lock the new rush in place and continue twisting.

After you've woven around the right rail, secure the rope at the back rail with a clothespin.

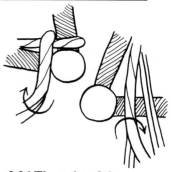

3.26 The twist of the rope should always be *away* from the post.

3.27 Make a long, smooth twist rather than a short, bumpy one.

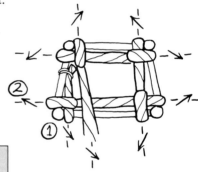

3.28 An exaggerated view of the twist.

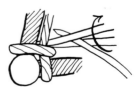

3.29 Adding a new rush to the rope. To keep the diameter of the rope consistent, new leaves need to be continually added to the rope. When weaving the gussets, you can add a new leaf, giving the rope a few tight twists to lock it into place.

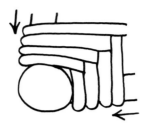

3.30 Use your fingers or a block of wood to crowd the rush together against the posts.

3.31 As you begin the regular rounds, add new leaves at the corner turns, leaving a 3- to 4-inch tail hanging below.

❖ Always twist away from the corner posts.

Begin the next round of the gusset. Start as before on the left and repeat, until all of the tied rushes are used up. Add a new rush to the last one or two tied rushes if they are too small to make rope of the right diameter. When you've used up the rushes from this bunch, tie their tails on the right rail. Wrap the string around the bundle of rushes, pull it tight, and take both ends of the string around the right rail four or five times. Tie the string with a square knot on the inside of the rail and cut the ends. Cut the rush behind the tie with an angling cut toward the corner post. Remove the clothespin and the rush tails. Save these rush ends to use for stuffing later on. If you have not yet woven as far as the pencil mark, tie another batch on the left rail a little farther back and repeat the whole process. You'll have to guesstimate how many rushes are needed, but try to have at least two rushes left over on the left rail after the pencil mark is reached for beginning the regular rounds.

As you did for the imitation rush chair, crowd the rush together against the posts to fill all the spaces. As natural rush is more

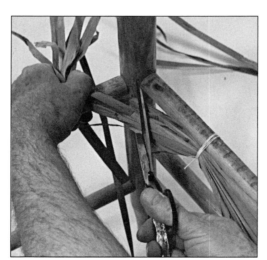

When you've used up the first bunch of rushes, tie the tails to the inside of the right rail and trim the ends.

prone to breakage than is imitation rush, use your fingers to crowd the rope into place (figure 3.30) instead of a hammer and screwdriver. If your fingers cannot crowd the rope tightly enough, you can use a wood block, held top and bottom and at a right angle to the rail, to crowd the rush firmly into place.

Filling in the Center

When you reach the pencil marks, tie off the tail ends on the right rail farther back than the first tie and trim them. Now use the two leftover rushes on the left rail to begin the regular rounds. Proceed as you did for the imitation rush chair, working around and around the chair (page 79). Frequently check the alignment of the round and be sure to make square corner turns. Do not let cross strands override. Your tension on the rope should be as firm as possible but not so tight as to break it. Experience will tell you how much it should be.

When you wove the gussets, you added new rushes into the twist of the cross strands. As you start to fill in the center, you can now add new leaves at the right-angle turns (figure 3.31). To do this, place the new rush directly in the corner with 3 or 4 inches hanging below, and twist the rope toward the center, that is, in the normal way, away from the post. Go around the rail, bring the rushes up in center, begin the next twisting, and give the tail just bypassed a good tug toward the corner post to keep the end out of the way in subsequent weaving. It is in adding new rush that making the turns away from the posts becomes important, as these twists are what lock the ends into place and prevent them from popping out.

Adding the Stuffing

Add the stuffing (page 80) when one-third of the seat has been woven. Park the weaver (figure 3.5) between two cross ropes and cut and install one layer of cardboard to fit the four top corner pockets. Turn the chair over, trim off the tails or loose ends to $1/4$ inch, and stuff the cut-off pieces into the underside corner pockets. If you fold the ends over, these scraps slide right in between the lower layer and the cardboard. Use the butt and stalk pile if more are needed. You'll stuff the center area when about two-thirds of the seat has been woven, at which time the stalks will fill the center gap. If the scrap supply has been depleted, fold up a whole rush for stuffing. You can use a dowel or stick to poke the rush into the pockets, but I find that my fingers are sufficient tools.

The purpose of the stuffing is to fill in the space between the top and bottom of the seat that is the depth of the rails. The stuffing

should be firmly packed and the bottom of the seat slightly bulged. After you've finished stuffing the bottom corner pockets, return to the top and continue weaving.

It is not necessary to put much twist into the rope that will be covered up with weaving later on, but I find that the rope remains neater and stronger if I twist it a hand's width beyond the rails. As you work, you will also appreciate the time and energy that you can save by twisting the rope only gently in non-public areas.

❖ To help maintain a consistent diameter, always add the butt end of a new leaf to the rope. Placing two butt ends together would make a bulge; conversely, piecing two tip ends together would cause a thin place in your rope.

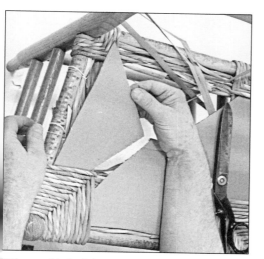

When a third of the seat has been woven, add cardboard triangles to the top corner pockets.

To press the seat upward, stuff the bottom corner pockets with pieces of waste rush.

❖ If your rush cracks and breaks a lot while you are working, it is an indication that your leaves aren't damp enough.

❖ If a leaf cracks as you are working, twist the rope tighter or looser to hide the crack on the underside.

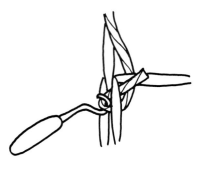

3.32 Starting the final knot.

Closing Up the Center

As the sides close up, pay special attention to alignment, as the sides must remain parallel. When you are ready to weave the figure eights, again trim the tails on the bottom and complete the stuffing of the bottom front and back pockets. As the center hole closes up, you'll need to use the buttonhook to pull the rush through to the top. Crowd the center figure eights together every three or four rounds by holding the screwdriver shaft vertically in the space, with one hand below and the other above, pulling firmly to the side. Straighten and crowd the rope loops on the rails. The last rope should be a very tight fit. Trim the tails. Tie twisted rope on the underside by using the buttonhook to pull the rope under a woven rush (figure 3.32). Pull rope under additional rushes to make a knot (figure 3.33).

Just before you begin weaving the figure eights, add more stuffing to the bottom pockets.

As the center closes up, you'll need to use the buttonhook to bring a loop of rope up through the center hole.

3.33 Secure the end by looping the end of the rope underneath the ropes around the center hole.

Crowd the rushes together firmly with your fingers.

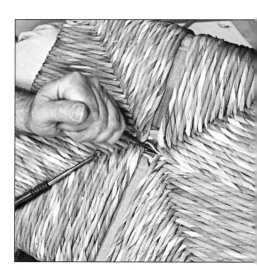

Enlarge the center hole with a screwdriver.

Secure the end by looping it under rushes around the center hole.

Cleanup

Cleanup follows a sigh of relief, accompanied by twinges in overworked arm muscles. Hose off the plastic drop cloth and hang it on a line to dry. Dry the unused rush. Mix it with fresh rush in the next job. Throwing dry rushes into the fireplace is a mistake as they make horrendous smoke.

Our cat friends sometimes discover that a natural rush seat, top or bottom, makes superb claw-sharpening material. We provide them with a scratching post, enhanced with a little catnip, as a diversion. Anything but our beautiful rush seat, please.

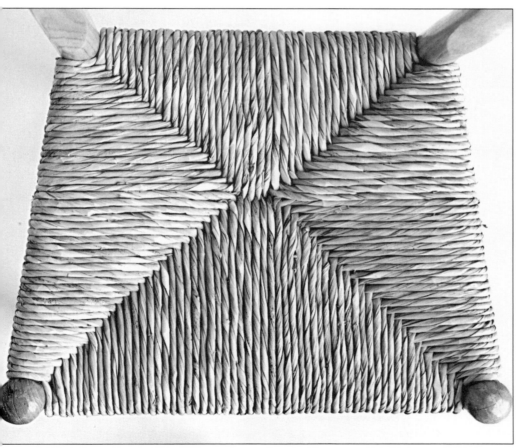

The finished seat.

Finishing

When you've finished the seat, immediately brush the top and bottom with boiled linseed oil (available at hardware stores). Let the oil soak in overnight and the next day coat the top and edges again. Drying time will be about a week. Using a solution of $2/3$ linseed oil and $1/3$ turpentine will cut drying time in half. Because the fumes of the turpentine will be very strong indoors, I recommend that you do this job outside. Six months later, give the seat another coat of oil. For the ultimate finish, apply another coat of linseed oil a year later. Preserved in this manner, your chair seat will last for a lifetime.

Between 1820 and 1840, many rush seats were coated with a thick, creamy solution of water-soluble glue and chalk powder called gesso. This finish made the seat very solid and boardlike; it must have been durable, as chairs with this treatment can still be found. Use gesso only where a match is necessary.

VARIATIONS
Notes About Stuffings

Sometimes in old chairs you'll find veneer cut to fit the top pockets (in place of cardboard). This makes an excellent stuffing and gives a smooth base for the rope to lie on. If it is still in good shape, you can reuse it on your new seat.

You'll also find old chair seats stuffed only with rush from the bottom, pushing the cross strands tight against the seat ropes. This method produces a seat that sags. You'll probably notice rushes broken along the rail. This problem can be avoided by using cardboard in the top pockets and rush stuffing in the bottom pockets.

Joining Rush

I've described two methods of joining rush: weaving a leaf into the twist (figure 3.29) and adding rush at the corner turns (figure 3.31). You can also join pieces with a square knot or a half hitch on the cross strand. The advantage of this method is that the new rush can't possibly slide out. The disadvantages are that it is time-consuming and the many joins necessary make the underside look messy indeed.

Weaving In Stages

Rush tends to relax and shrink across its diameter as it dries on the seat. This can be counteracted, to a degree, by weaving the seat in quarters over a week's time. The previous dried weaving can be crowded tighter together as the new is put in. It requires dampening a small batch of rush daily. I always weave a seat in one day, and I find that I get good results by paying close attention to detail: the rush must not be dripping wet, the rope must be twisted firmly, the tension must be maximal, and the strands must be crowded very closely without overlapping.

Creative Rope Twisting

Unlike imitation rush, which is uniform in diameter throughout its length, natural rush rope can be judiciously increased or diminished as needed. For example, while you are weaving the figure eights, you notice that the space at the front rail is a little larger than the space in the middle of the seat. You can correct for this by increasing the diameter of the rope as it goes over the front rail. To do this, cut the butt of a smaller rush at a 30-degree ngle. Insert this end in the twist an inch or so back from the rail (figure 3.34) and conceal the end completely in the twist. By spreading this gain over six or more ropes, the space is filled and is imperceptible.

Should the center of the weaving bulge while space still remains to be filled along the rails (figure 3.35), you can sometimes save

the situation by thickening the twist along the rails and twisting more tightly in the center. Far better is prevention, and attention to correct technique. Have the right-angle turns collapsed because of overriding cross strands? Are the turns sharp? Is the twist too fat in the middle and too thin at the rail? Is the tension too loose?

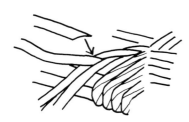

3.34 To increase the rope diameter to gain on the front rail, you can add new leaves as the rope approaches the front rail.

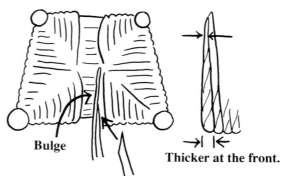

Bulge

Thicker at the front.

3.35 If the center bulges, you can increase the diameter of the twist along the rails.

Interrupted Rushing

For temporary stops in the middle of a job, clip the working rope, at the base of the twist, to the seat with a clothespin, or loop the rope between cross strands and leave as is. Leaving work overnight requires more attention. Clip the rope to the seat, fold up the rush ends and cover them with a small plastic bag to which 2 tablespoons of water have been added. Tie the bag securely shut and tuck the bag between strands or in a corner pocket. The rushes will stay damp enough to continue in the morning. In an emergency, this "hold" may be left for one more day.

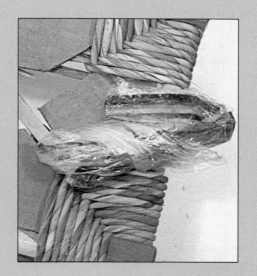

When Reverse Twists Meet

As the seat closes, there will be four places where the ropes lying alongside one another twist in opposite directions (at the sides and in front and back where the figure eights meet). Although this is a natural consequence of this technique, you can plan the meeting point of the twists to make them less obtrusive. I find that they are least conspicuous when they meet at the side. As you weave the figure eights, simply continue the twist of the rope as you work toward one edge (figure 3.36). The other alternative is for the twists to meet in the center. Mark the center point on the front rail and work your twists toward this point, then reverse them (figure 3.37). The direction of these twists shouldn't concern you; only the most experienced rusher will ever notice.

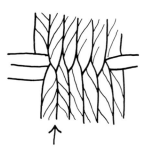

3.36 The most unobtrusive point for twists in opposite directions to meet is at the side.

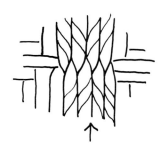

3.37 You can position the point at which the twists meet in the center by reversing the twist on one rope when the center is reached.

OTHER MATERIALS AND TOOLS

If your patience is of generous proportions, you can make a seat out of corn shucks. A small project like a stool is most suitable, as the husks are hardly a foot long. The inner husks make an almost white seat. The supply is unlimited and free. Another possible material is raffia, a member of the palm family. Used as a protective covering for chianti bottles, raffia's fine silky texture makes an attractive blond seat for small children's or dollhouse chairs.

If your patience stretches still more, there are rush-type seats traditional in France and Italy that are made with a core of grass or sedges wrapped with wheat straw, each rope wrapped individually as it is woven. The spectacular result is shining and golden. It wears fairly well if painted with linseed oil. When the alternatives have been weighed, however, natural rush holds its own at the top of the heap without any trouble at all.

SPLINT

CHAPTER IV

**Hickory Splint
Ash, Oak, and Flat
    Rattan Splint
Cloth and Leather
Tape Seats
Paper Splint**

*A well-worn hickory chair seat on an antique Shaker chair. Chair courtesy of
Verna J. Hames.*

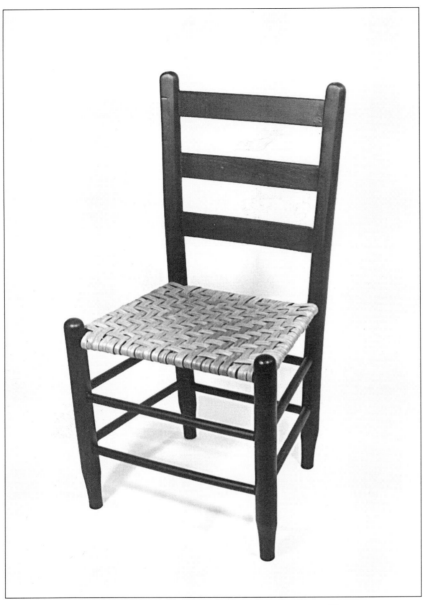

A ladder-back chair with a hickroy splint seat woven in a twill pattern. Owner: the author.

Traditionally, splint chair seats were woven with long lengths of thin pieces of oak, ash, or hickory which had been laboriously hand-split from tree trunks. Today, the term splint refers to the technique of weaving chair seats with wood splints, but it also includes other materials such as rattan, cloth tapes, and paper.

In splint chair seats, a warp is wound between the front and the back rails, and a weft is woven across at right angles between the side rails, weaving both the top and the bottom of the seat. You'll find splint chair seats almost exclusively on country primitive ladder-back or mule-ear chairs with slightly sloping side rails and round rails on all four sides.

A twill weave in an over-two, under-two, or an over-three, under-three pattern is used for splint chair seats. You'll recognize twill by the pattern's definite diagonal line, and the splints cross over more than one splint at a time. As wood splints are stiff and brittle, a twill weave, which does not make the splint bend so much as it weaves in and out, eases the weaving and increases the length of time the chair will wear. The exception to this is in Shaker chair seats in which woven fabric tapes are used. Because this material is more flexible, than wood it can more easily weave in and out. Traditionally, Shaker seats were woven in a checkerboard, a one-over, one-under pattern called plain weave.

HICKORY SPLINT

Genuine hickory splint is the material of choice for any respectable country primitive ladder-back or mule-ear chair. Its dense grain makes for extreme durability, and its appearance is most compatible with the style of these chairs. As hickory splint is very hard to find, most suppliers stock more readily obtained substitutes such as ash, oak, and rattan splints. None of these will last as long as hickory. A do-it-yourselfer can make hickory splint from a fresh-cut tree trunk. *Making a Chair from a Tree* by Alexander (see Bibliography) will tell you how. But if it's not the right season (spring), and if you don't have a hickory tree handy, you may have to fall back on the materials that are available year-round from suppliers. Ash or rattan splints, or slab rattan (like 6 mm cane only larger, 8 mm to 10 mm wide) can be used on common rustic hickory porch furniture or on contemporary mule-ear chairs of no distinction. But for a good New England ladder-back or a refined Shaker, I would insist on genuine hickory splints.

Tools and Materials

Hickory can be ordered in widths of about $^1/_2$ to $^3/_4$ inch. Narrower is better because it will leave smaller gaps in the finished seat due to shrinkage in the width of the splint. Wider sizes benefit from being woven in stages to minimize the problem of shrinkage across the width (discussed later). The

method given here is done in one sitting using $^1/_2$-inch-wide hickory splint. One chair seat will take about two pounds of material, or about 60 to 120 linear feet, depending on the width.

The tools required for splint weaving are minimal. You'll need sturdy scissors for cutting off the old chair seat and for cutting joins, a dull table knife will come in handy for coaxing through splints in tight places. You'll also need flat-headed nails, a small hammer, and a sharp knife for cutting holes for the joins. A pail, or something to soak your hickory in, will also be needed. You may find a low stool or table to put your chair on saves your back while you're working.

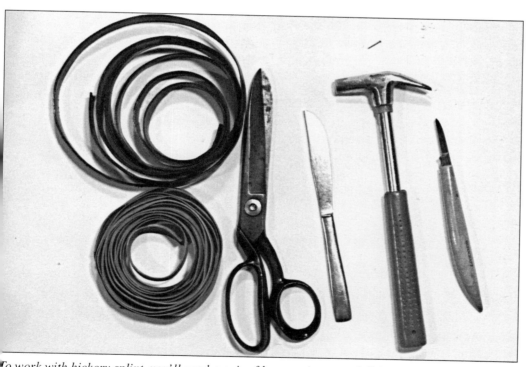

To work with hickory splint, you'll need a pair of heavy scissors, a dull kitchen knife, a small hammer, and a small sharp knife. We'll use $^1/_2$-inch hickory splint, soaked until it is as flexible as leather. One chair will take about two pounds of splint.

Preparation

Choosing the longest lengths to start, soak three or four splint coils until they bend easily, like leather (about 30 to 45 minutes). When the splint is flexible, remove two lengths from the water and add two more coils. The wood-grain side is public, the back is smooth. Hickory is so tough that either end can be woven without fraying.

Winding the Warps

On this style of chair the side rails slope gently from the front to the back, making the front rail longer than the back. In order to weave a square pattern, you must impose a rectilinear shape on the trapezoidal seat (see Chapter III, page 75). Measure the length of the back rail between the two corner posts and mark the distance, centered, on the front rail. Unlike the seat woven with rush, the main body of a splint seat is woven first. The gussets are filled in later.

Begin by wrapping the warps between the front and back rails. Start on the left side of the chair, and take one end of the splint over and around the back rail and nail it one-third of the way back from the front rail on the inside of the left side rail. Wrap the end of the splint over the front rail, lining up the left edge with the pencil mark. Go across the bottom, up around the back rail, then across the top. Continue to wrap in this way, around and around, forming a double layer of splint. Crowd the splints very close together. Keep the tension medium or less, as the cross weaving (weft) will tighten up the warps plenty.

When one length of splint runs out, make a join on the bottom of the seat with a traditional arrow-and-slot technique (figure 4.1). Cut the arrow on the old splint with scissors and cut the slot on the new splint with the knife, then put the arrow through the slot to secure the join. String, wire, hog rings, and staples are a disgrace in splicing this fine material.

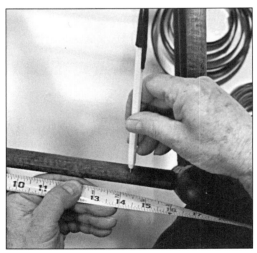

To define the central rectangle of a seat with sloping side rails, mark the width of the back onto the front rail. The center is woven first and the gussets are filled in later.

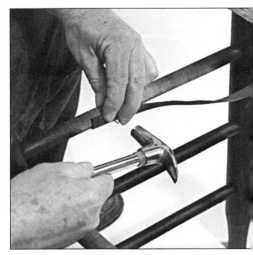

Nail either end of the hickory splint to the inside of the left side rail.

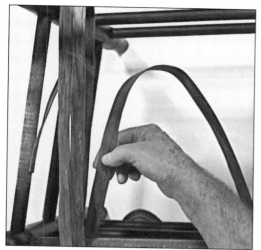

Begin wrapping from the back to the front, lining up the left edge of the splint with the mark on the front rail. Wrap around and around until you reach the mark near the right end of the front rail. Use only enough tension to keep the splint flat, and crowd the hickory tightly together as you wrap.

Begin a warp join on the underside, cutting an arrow on the old splint with scissors.

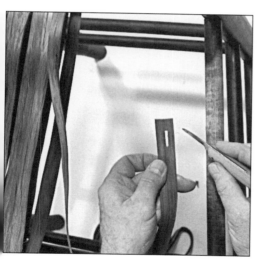

With a knife, cut a slot near the end of the new splint.

Push the arrow up through the slot and turn it to lock it into position.

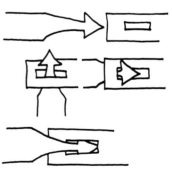

4.1 Join a new length of splint on the bottom with an arrow and slot. Cut the arrow with scissors and the slot with a knife, then put the arrow through the slot to secure the join.

Continue to wrap the warps until a splint over the front rail lies approximately one empty width to the left of the pencil mark on the right side of the front rail. Take this weaver across the underside of the seat, around and over the back rail to fill the space up to the corner post. Take the splint down in front of the corner post, and under and over the right rail, keeping the wood-grain side to the outside.

Hold the join for a moment as you continue to wind the seat.

At the back right post, bring the splint up and around to fill the last space on the back rail.

Take the splint in front of the corner post in the back right corner, down through the corner, and up around the right rail. This splint is now ready to act as weft; make sure it is long enough to reach beyond the left rail.

Weaving the Weft

You are now ready to weave the first weft row right to left (figure 4.2) with this leftover length of weaver. This splint must be long enough to weave across the entire seat. If it's not, go back to the last warp pass and add a new length on the underside of the chair. Weave over the first warp, then under two, over two across the seat until you reach the left rail. Go around the left rail and turn the chair upside down to weave across the bottom. Weave around and around to form one layer on the top of the seat and another on the bottom.

On the bottom, weave over one, then under three, over three across. You could weave over and under two on the bottom as you did on the top, but the weaving is apt to get very tight. Join weavers on the bottom by overlapping the splint almost the width of the seat (figure 4.3), instead of the arrow-and-slot joins you made in the warp.

When you've completed this first row across the underside, turn the chair upright again. On the top, weave a twill pattern as

The first row of weft. Weave this splint over the first warp, then under two, over two across the seat.

4.2 When the weaver approaches the right-hand pencil mark on the front rail, take it across the underside of the seat, under and over the back rail, down in front of the corner post, and under and over the right rail, to become the first weft row right to left.

Take the splint around the left rail, and turn the chair upside down. Weave over the first warp then under three, over three across the underside.

Turn the chair upright again and insert the second weft on the top. Offset the weave one strand by going over the first two warps, and continue across in the under-two, over-two pattern.

4.3 Make weft joins on the bottom by overlapping the splint almost the width of the seat.

shown in the drawing (figure 4.4). Offset the second weft one warp from the pattern of the first weft by weaving over the first two warps, instead of one as you did in the first row. As before, continue weaving under two, over two across the seat. On the underside, offset the weave one warp and weave over three, under three (figure 4.5).

On the underside, again offset the pattern one strand and weave across in the under-three, over-three pattern.

With a dull kitchen knife, pack the splints tightly together.

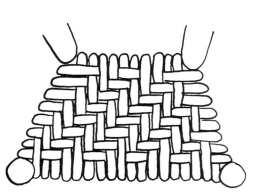

4.4 Weave an over-two, under-two twill pattern on the top of the seat.

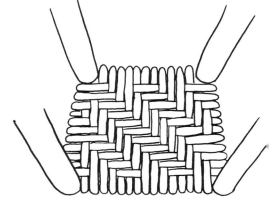

4.5 On the bottom, offset one warp and weave over three, under three.

Weaving the Gussets

After about half the wefts have been woven, fill in part of each gusset, weaving front to back with short lengths of splint. Use a kitchen knife to help slide the splint through

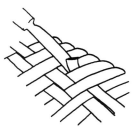

4.6 Use a kitchen knife to help slide the splint through.

Fill in the gussets with short strips of splint, tucking in the ends.

Use the kitchen knife to help force in the last few splints.

(figure 4.6). The first splint in the right gusset should be cut square, and the end should touch the right back upright so that the splint covers the gap left when the warp became the weft (figure 4.7). To end the other warps in the gusset, simply tuck each end under a weft splint.

Continue weaving the seat, crowding the splints firmly together. If by the time you're completing the final front rows, the warps have dried out too much to be flexible, dampen the front area with a wet towel. Fill in the last short warps in the gusset left and right, and add a final splint across the front if needed, tucking the ends in neatly.

This job should be completed rapidly to get the full benefit of the damp, workable splint. After the seat has dried for several days, the splint will shrink in width, which will cause a gap of $^1/_{16}$ to $^3/_{32}$ inch between the strands, or more with wider splint. (Unlike cane, hickory shrinks very little in length.) Many antiques display this characteristic gap, which may be $^1/_8$ inch wide or wider if the splint is wide.

If the space at the front needs to be filled but a regular splint is too wide, make a narrower one with scissors.

4.7 Cut the first splint in the right gusset to cover the gap left when the warp became the weft.

Weaving In Stages

Some caners believe that shrinkage can be minimized by weaving the splint over a period of several days so that dried weaving can be crowded closer together before each new section is put in. Take care at the warp joins not to break the dried arrows off with the weaver. Dampen the working area with a wet towel to assist in getting the weaver through. The trouble with this technique is that the last few splints will shrink; let's just decide the gaps are characteristic and attractive and be happy with that.

A hickory splint seat is rough at first, but soon wears smooth. The fine patina on an old seat is a credit to this beautiful material.

Finishing Hickory Splint

Mix three parts boiled linseed oil (available at hardware stores) with one part turpentine. Paint the splint with one coat of this mixture and then wipe it off thoroughly with a rag. Oil alone makes sticky, glassy spots because the wood is so hard.

The roughness of the new hickory splint seat will soon wear down to a fine patina, and gaps between the splints will open as the seat dries.

ASH, OAK, AND FLAT RATTAN SPLINT

Ash or oak splint and flat rattan are woven like hickory. They tend to become brittle rather quickly, especially if exposed outdoors, so be prepared for a relatively short life. Shrinkage is minimal, however. These materials are readily available from cane supply houses (in contrast to hickory splint) and the price is relatively modest. The Caning Shop in Berkeley, California, provides a helpful table in their catalog for the quantities required for a job. For example, a seat 15 by 12 inches needs 120 linear feet of $^1/2$-inch-wide splint. A 1-pound bunch of flat reed splint $^1/2$ inch wide contains 185 linear feet.

These materials are "directional". Bend a wet length over your finger, trying both sides. The fibers will rise on the wrong side. The fibers point toward the tie end; the other is the weaving end (figure 4.8). Weaving with the wrong end will result in fearsome tearing during weaving.

To make warp joins on the underside of the seat, overlap the ends about 4 inches, hold them firmly together, notch and then tie them together with crochet thread or other fairly fine string (figure 4.9). The arrow and slot won't do; these materials will split. Make weft joins by overlapping on the underside of the seat without tying.

Do the weaving in one sitting, if possible. Try to complete the whole job while the splint is damp and flexible. On a large job such as a porch swing, which may take three days to do, dampen the woven splint with a wet towel before you resume work to avoid snapping a dry warp in two. Your language when this happens is apt to be frightful.

Finishing Ash, Oak, and Rattan Splints

Stain the splint first if desired, and let the stain dry. Then paint the seat with one coat of boiled linseed oil. Varnish is not a good choice as it makes these materials brittle.

4.8 Finding the weaving end on ash, oak, and flat rattan splints. Bend a wet length over your finger, trying both sides. On the wrong side, the fibers point toward the tie end; the other is the weaving end.

4.9 Make warp joins with oak, ash, and flat rattan by overlapping the ends about 4 inches, notching them and then tying them together.

CLOTH AND LEATHER TAPE SEATS

True American masterpieces, genuine Shaker chairs and rockers often had cloth tape seats. The original tapes were worsted wool handwoven on a small loom. Joins were made by sewing the tapes together. Nowadays, replacement tape is machine-made cotton in a choice of widths and colors. It can be woven on the chair in a plain weave, over one, under one, for a cheerful checkerboard pattern, or in a twill. Natural rush and hickory splints are equally authentic materials for Shaker chairs, and either of these choices will give longer wear than woven tape.

Before beginning to weave the seat, the Shakers made a stuffing pad from a square of muslin with cotton batting sewn to the center area. The muslin flaps were then glued to the four rails before the seat weaving began. The woven seat completely covered this stuffing on both top and bottom, while the pad added comfort and minimized sagging.

For a Spanish or southwestern flavor, $^1/2$-inch or wider leather strips can be woven dry. They can also be lightly dampened, not soaked, and then they will shrink as tight as new shoes. Weave the pattern and make the joins the same as for hickory splint. The final result is durable and handsome. Rawhide, cut into strips and thoroughly soaked, makes an extremely strong seat, but handling the wet, slimy strips may turn you off. The finished product won't win any beauty prizes either. And Fido will find the seat fascinating to chew on, an added hazard. However, fine Moroccan leather is an excellent alternative. Be sure you are sitting down when you price it at the leather shop.

PAPER SPLINT

Paper splint has a niche, perhaps in children's furniture, but it does not belong on a Shaker chair. It is woven dry. Probably the speediest of all seating materials, it might be just the thing for 200 stools.

Paper splint can be left unfinished or can be painted with shellac, varnish, or lacquer.

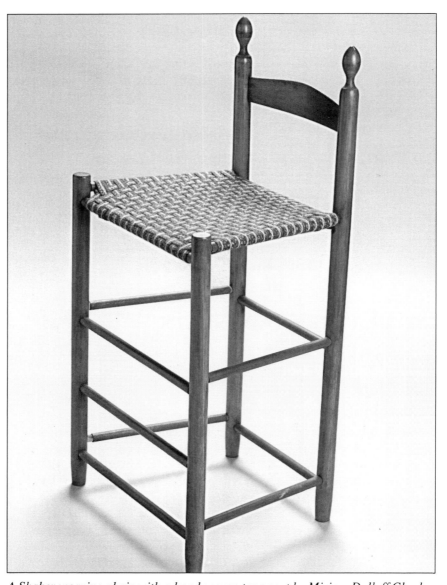

A Shaker weaving chair with a hand-woven tape seat by Miriam Dolloff Chesley.

WIDE CANE
CHAPTER V

Tools and Materials
Preparation
Wide Cane Twill Seat
  Weaving a chair back
  Multiple weavers
A Basket-Weave
  Chair Seat

A walnut Eastlake style rocker with matched veneer on the top slat is woven in 6 mm cane in a 4/4 twill pattern. Courtesy of Inez Gamble.

❖ Some old rockers use narrower cane size and a shortened stitch; 4 and 5 mm cane can be woven over three and under three, although 5 mm gets rather tight. A 3/3 twill with 6 mm cane is possible, but the rails had better be strong. Four mm cane in a 2/2 twill is a possibility, just barely, but the tightness is excruciating, forcing the caner's patience into bankruptcy.

Wide cane is 4, 5, or 6 mm cane that is normally too large for seat weaving in the traditional cane pattern. Like splint, the technique for weaving with wide cane involves two sets of elements, the warp which is usually wrapping from front to back and the weft which weaves perpendicular to the warp.

Wide cane in a closely woven twill (see page 124 for more on weaves) makes a very durable seat. This technique is also called double cane because it has two layers of cane in the weaving, similar to splint and rush. Because wide cane is woven around the outside of the frame, the construction of the chair or stool must be sturdy enough to withstand the cane shrinkage when it dries. Like chair cane, 6 mm cane has a slight shrinkage over its length as it dries, much the same as chair cane does. The shrinkage in width is so small as to be unnoticeable. The cane is further tightened by weaving the twill pattern, each row being jammed tight against the previous row. At the conclusion of weaving, the cane

has developed considerable pressure on the seat rails, which will snap if not sturdy enough.

Seat rails less than 1 inch in diameter are likely to break, a disastrous consequence. Wide cane adapts well to furniture made of steel tubing where strength is no problem. It is found most often on porch rockers or Kennedy rockers with caned seat and back. These rockers may have back side rails made of 3/4-inch dowels which fit into heavy head and bottom rails. These types benefit from a 1/4-by-1-inch slat let into grooves in the dowels at the horizontal center line. It either straightens previously bowed dowels or prevents their pulling inward with the new cane. Other old rockers have an inner back frame that was originally woven separate from the chair. Usually these can be rewoven without dismantling the chair, but if the inner frame sits tight against the back post, you'll have to take the chair apart. Wide cane is suitable for chairs with knees (braces at the inner corners of the

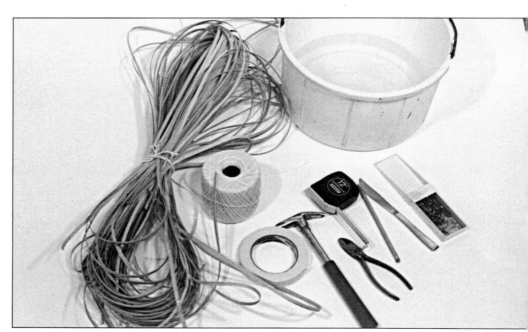

Materials for working wide cane: scissors, a kitchen knife, flat-headed nails and a small hammer, side-cutting pliers, masking tape, string, a tape measure, and a hank of 6 mm cane.

:at frame) as the cane covers them up. If
:eeded, you can add knees to strengthen
:oubtful rails.

Wide cane, rush, and splint are ordinarily
:iterchangeable materials for a seat with slop-
:ig side rails. We have already seen the tradi-
:onal pattern for both imitation and natural

rush on this type of chair seat, and we have
worked the twill pattern in splint. Although
other weaves sometimes appear in 6 mm
cane, the twill pattern gives maximum
strength and is the preferred one for the majority of jobs.

TOOLS AND MATERIALS

Six mm cane usually is found on large
:hairs and hefty porch rockers with commodi-
:us seat and backs. Six mm cane is also used
:or wrapping the decorative additions to rat-
:in furniture. Usually the cane covers the
:inctures of the large rattan structural pieces.
:' you do caning for any length of time, you
:ill find yourself rewrapping quantities of rat-
:in furniture, particularly bar stools.

Four mm cane might be the proper scale
:or a child's rocker woven in a twill pattern. It
:ould probably be too fine and too weak for

an adult seat 24 inches wide. Five mm cane
often turns up on Danish chairs, some woven
in basket weave and others in an open, over-
and-under weave with fancy edges.

Wide cane is purchased in 500-foot hanks.
You'll need one hank for an average-sized
seat. In addition, you'll need a bucket for
soaking the cane, scissors for cutting off the
old seat, a kitchen knife, flat-headed nails,
side-cutting pliers, a small hammer, masking
tape, strings, and a measuring tape.

PREPARATION

Wide cane is worked wet. Soak four or
:ve cane lengths at a time until they are pli-
:ble, remove and replace them with another
:atch as you work.

As with hand cane, always keep the shiny
:de up (see page 15) and work with the weav-
:ig end, not the tie end (see page 15). Long
:ane strands are best for wrapping the warp
:ont to back. Short ones are worked in the
:eft to make the pattern. A hank of cane with
:ll short lengths is cause for loud noises to the
:pplier, as they increase our work a great
:mount.

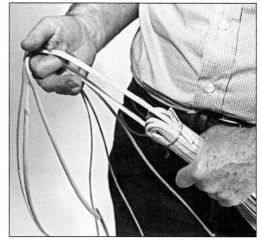

*Pull a few strands of cane from the folded end
of the hank and soak them.*

5.1 Make joins with wide cane the same as for ash splint: overlap the ends about 4 inches on the underside of the seat, hold them firmly together, notch and then tie them.

5.2 One cane width before the right rear corner, bring the last strand from the underside over the rear rail, down in front of the corner post, and up around the right rail snug against the post. Weave across the top and then across the underside going over four, under four. To start the second row on top, go over one more warp than on the previous row, then under four, over four.

WIDE CANE TWILL SEAT

Refer to the step-by-step photos for splint, pages 100–101, as the method of weaving is about the same; the joins are like those for ash splint (figure 5.1). Mark the back post width on the front rail to define the central rectangle of the seat.

Warping

To begin the twill pattern, take the tie end of the wet cane over the back rail and nail it to the midpoint of the inner left rail. Wrap the cane over the front rail, across the bottom, across the top, and so on as for hickory splint, keeping the strands close together. Wrap only tight enough so that the cane lies flat. For joins, overlap the ends about 4 inches on the underside of the seat, hold them firmly together, notch and then tie them (figure 5.1). Keep the joins away from the rails. Cotton crochet thread is best for the ties but any strong, thin string will do. Staples are not good; they let go at unexpected times and tend to split the cane.

One cane width before the right rear corner, bring the last strand from the underside over the rear rail, filling in the last cane width, down in front of the corner post, and up around the right rail snug against the post (figure 5.2). This cane starts the weft. Plan ahead so that it is a long one.

Weaving the Weft

For a wide cane seat, I prefer a 4/4 twill pattern; it is strong and beautiful, and the larger interlacement makes a looser weave which puts less pressure on the rails as the cane dries and shrinks. This pattern is similar to the 2/2 twill we made with splint, except that the pattern is enlarged by going over four, under four. We will further reduce the pressure by weaving a 4/4 basket weave on the underside.

Weave over the first two warps to begin the pattern, then under four, over four across the seat until you reach the left rail. Turn the chair upside down or on its back (a good-sized low table is handy for this) and weave across the bottom, over four, under four. Set

the chair up to weave the second row on top (figure 5.2). Here the weaver goes over one more warp than it did in the previous row, then under four, over four. Push down the correct warps to slide the weaver through; a little upward hook on the weaver helps. You could use a coat hanger wire, straightened out, to weave across, holding the warps apart, then slide the cane through next to it, but I find that fingers can do the job much faster and the wire is useless at the front when things get tight.

Take the cane across the underside the same as on the first row. On the underside weave four rows with the same over-under pattern and then reverse the pattern, going under where you went over, and so on, for the next four rows. This results in a large checkerboard pattern (figure 5.3) which diminishes the pressure of the cane on the rails; it's also a time-saver and it doesn't show.

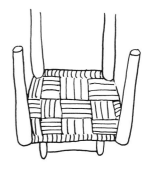

5.3 Take the cane across the underside the same as on the first row. Do four rows the same and then reverse the next four rows.

On the top, follow the pattern shown in figure 5.4. Note how row 4 begins; the weaver goes *under* the first warp. If you are unsure where to start as you begin each row, decide where the next strand should come up and count back four warps to decide where it should go down.

At first, crowd the rows together with your fingers. Later a dull kitchen knife will do the job, as well as help slide the weaver through. Crowd the rows back with a good amount of force and keep them straight.

Make joins in the weft by overlapping on the top weaving (figure 5.5). End the old cane on the top, take the tie end of the new cane in backward, duplicating several stitches already completed. Hold a 1-inch tail of this fresh cane with your right hand and a loop of cane in the left as you slide it onto the top of the previous row. The overlap should be 3 to 4 inches long. Trim the tail closely. The next row of weaving will lock the overlap in tightly.

5.4 Row 4 begins with the weaver going under the first warp.

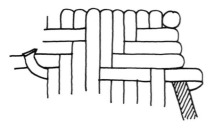

5.5 To join a new weft strand, end the old cane on the top and take the tie end of the new cane in backward, duplicating several stitches already completed. The overlap should be 3 to 4 inches long.

Weaving the Gussets

When you've woven a third to a half of the seat, fill in two or three canes in each gusset, weaving front to back. Leave the tails hanging out at the front, long to enough to reach the back rail on the underside, then turn the chair over and weave the tails in one at a time, inner ones first. They don't have to follow the bottom pattern strictly but should alternate so that they are locked in firmly. Trim the ends and tuck them under a convenient cross cane. These ends become progressively shorter on the sloping sides.

Continue the weft until you reach the front rail. The cane will be very tight. Dampen the working area with a wet cloth and use the dull kitchen knife for every stitch. Close up the gussets on the sides with short scraps, weaving front to back. On some chairs an additional row or two of weft at the front may be needed. Cut the ends of these canes and tuck them neatly under warp canes on the left and right front corners.

WEAVING A DIAMOND PATTERN

A straight twill pattern is a standard treatment for wide cane. After some experience with straight twill, you can do a twill diamond pattern for the top of a seat or the front of a back panel (figure 5.6). Start with a square or rectangular panel, if possible, and draw the entire pattern on squared paper to act as a guide. Each vertical column on the paper will represent one warp, and each horizontal row will represent one weft. Wrap the warp on the seat or back panel, count the strands, and mark off that many columns on your paper. Mark the center lines, both vertical and horizontal, on your paper diagram. Draw the pattern from the center out in each direction.

With masking tape, mark the center points of the back, the front, and each side of the seat or back panel to show where the pattern reverses. Then follow your diagram as you weave, checking to be sure your pattern reverses in the center. On the center lines, there will be a place where a maximum of five canes are spanned in a stitch. When you have woven the weft down to the center mark on the side rails, reverse the pattern.

On a tall rectangle, the pattern still reverses in the center of each side, or you may place the center diamond several rows above or below the exact middle by reversing wherever you wish along the side rails.

Weaving a diamond demands close attention but, like bricks, the pattern is laid in a row at a time. Mistakes are terribly visible and should be corrected immediately. Have fun, and don't get lost.

5.6 The diamond pattern reverses on both the vertical and the horizontal center lines.

Weaving a Chair Back

To weave a chair back in wide cane, use the twill pattern on both sides. When it is complete, some of the string ties will be visible on the warp strands, although most will be buried. Use the small side-cutting pliers to nip the string and pull it out. Closely trim the cane stubs. The joins will become almost invisible, and the tight weave will hold them securely in place.

Multiple Weavers

Old chairs sometimes exhibit four weavers going around at the same time (figure 5.7). On a chair back, they start at the lower rail with the first weaver 2 inches in from the right rail, the second, 4 inches, the third, 6 inches, the fourth, 8 inches, depending on the width of the back. They go up to the right rail at an angle, around the right rail, and straight across the front. The front pattern is straight with the world and the back is skewed. Perhaps four weavers are a time-saver, but the single weaver looks much better.

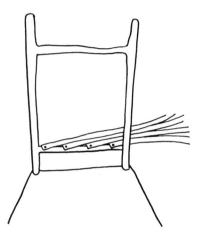

5.7 Some old chairs have four weavers going around at the same time. On a back panel, they start at the lower back rail in staggered positions and go up to the right rail at an angle. All four strands go around the right rail and weave straight across the front.

The finished chair seat.

A BASKET-WEAVE CHAIR SEAT

A porch rocker of contemporary design woven with 6 mm cane. Courtesy of Vicki Matthews.

Although the twill pattern gives maximum strength and is preferred for most jobs, you may need to duplicate a basket-weave pattern as in our sample chair. Here the original basket weave had its warp running side to side rather than the usual front to back, so we will duplicate that. The pattern works fine either way, so you are always free to turn it 90 degrees if needed.

Mark the width of the back rail onto the front rail to define the central rectangle of the seat. We will use these marks later when we weave the weft.

Cut off the old seat, noting the pattern so that you can duplicate it. On this seat, the warp went side to side rather than the usual front to back. When the frame is bare, mark the width of the back rail on the front rail.

Winding the Warp

A pair of warps is the backbone of the basket-weave pattern, though that pair is really a single strand wrapped twice. To begin wrapping the warp side to side, take the tie end of the cane under the left rail and nail it on the inner back rail. Bring the weaving end over the left rail, across the seat, and over the right rail. This strand should be snug to the back posts. Take it to the left across the underside, around the left rail, and to the right again making a pair of top strands at medium tension. Wrap twice around the right rail (figure 5.8). Now go across the underside again and make two wraps around the left rail (figure 5.9). This is the basic pattern of the warp: two warp strands across, separated by two wraps on each rail. Continue this pattern across the seat to the front rail.

As you are wrapping the warp, make joins on the inside of a side rail. Loosen the last wrap on the inside of a side rail and slip about 1½ inches of the tie end of the new cane be-

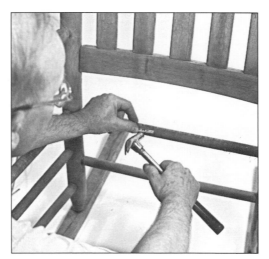

Nail the tie end of the cane to the inside of the back rail.

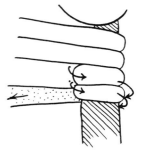

5.8 For a basket-weave warp, wrap twice across the entire seat, then twice around the right rail. Go back to the left on the underside of the seat.

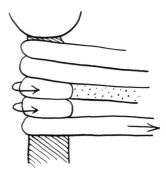

5.9 On the left rail, make two wraps. Continue with two wraps across, then two wraps on each rail.

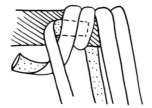

5.10 Loosen the last wrap on a side rail and slip about 1¹/₂ inches of the tie end of the new cane beneath this wrap.

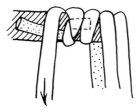

5.11 Pull the wrap tight again, make a twist with the old and new ends as shown in figure 5.10, and continue the wrapping with the new end.

neath this wrap (figure 5.10). Pull the wrap tight again, make a twist with the old and new ends (figure 5.11), and continue the wrapping with the old end. Make the next wrap catch the tie end of the new cane to hold it securely.

The second warp of the last pair at the front must be a long strand that ends at the right front post. Nail the end to the inner face of the front rail, or tie it temporarily to the front post or a chair rung and then, when the weft is done, weave it across the bottom of the seat and tuck it in.

Wind the warp across the seat, around the side rails, and across the underside. Wrap two strands across the top and then make two wraps for spacers on the right rail.

Return across the underside and make two wraps on the left rail. Repeat this pattern for the rets of the warp.

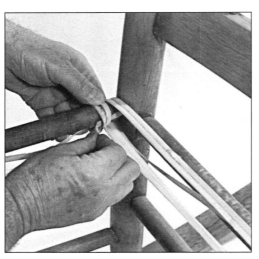

To start a new cane in the warp, loosen the last spacer wrap and tuck in the tie end of a new cane.

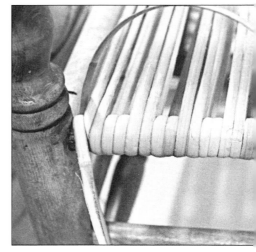

When you have finished winding the warp, temporarily secure the end at the right front rail. Weave it later, after you've woven the weft.

Weaving the Weft

Turn the chair upside down to begin the weft. Weave the tie end of a new strand across the underside from back to front, going over the first pair of warps, under the next pair, and so on. End this strand simply by tucking in the end. Further weaving on each side of it will hold it tightly in place.

Turn the chair upright. Bring the weaving end up around the back rail, snug against the back right post, and weave it from back to front, going over the first pair of warps, under the next pair, and so on to the mark on the front rail. Line it up with its right edge touching the mark.

Go around the front rail and turn the chair upside down. On the underside, go over one pair and under the next, opposite to the path of the previous weft. On top, row 2 goes under the first warp pair, over the second pair, and so on across the chair. Continue to weave the top and underside around and around.

On the underside, the warp pairs are not parallel; they form one pair at the right rail and then split to join other pairs at the left rail, so weave half the bottom with the pairs as they were joined at the right rail. When half the bottom is woven, begin using pairs as they group themselves on the left rail (figure 5.12). Make weft joins by overlapping on the underside of the seat. End the weft by burying the end, or simply nail the end to a convenient rail.

5.12 Weave half the bottom with the pairs as they were joined at the right rail. At the midpoint, begin using pairs as they group themselves on the left rail.

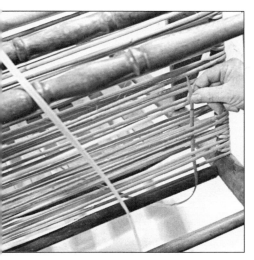

Turn the chair on its back to start the weft by weaving across the bottom, back to front. With the tie end of a new cane, weave over two, under two. Simply end this cane at the front of the warp, without any nail, tie, or other attachment. The weaving around it will hold it in place when the chair is completed.

Turn the chair over. With the weaving end, weave across the top from back to front going over the first pair of warps, under the next pair, and so on. Line up the cane with the mark on the front rail.

Turn the chair on its back. Take the weaver around the front rail and across the underside, going over-under the warp pairs opposite to the first pass.

The half basket-weave pattern has a single strand of weft going over and under pairs of warp. Add new cane by overlapping new and old weavers.

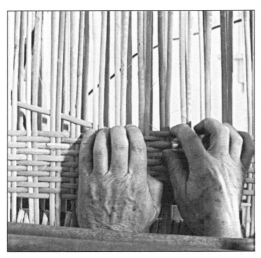

Straighten the weft with your fingers as you weave.

At the center of the seat on the underside, change the warp pairs by moving over one to make new groupings.

Weaving the Gussets

Fill the gussets with short lengths as for the splint chair, tucking in the ends. Front top-side filler rows are optional, as in the twill pattern, but here the ends should be anchored with a spot of glue to keep them in place.

A basket-weave back follows the same layout with two vertical warps and two spacers. The front panel is uniform but the back side requires a shift of the weaver at midpoint, like the underside of the seat, due to the angling warps (figure 5.12).

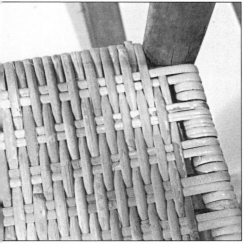

At any time during the weaving of the seat, you can go back and fill in the right gusset with short pieces of cane. End each piece simply by tucking it in.

If the space between the last warp and the front rail seems too wide, you can fill it in with short canes. Use the kitchen knife to help get the cane through the tight space.

Cut the cane at the front posts and tuck in the ends.

Weave the left gusset, inserting several short canes to fill the space on the top before you turn the chair on its back to weave each of the short ends across the underside of the gusset.

Adding a Filler

To complete the job, weave a row on the front underside and bury the end. Front topside filler rows are optional, as in the twill pattern, but if you use them, the ends should be anchored with a spot of glue to keep them in place.

Finishing

No finishing is needed unless stain is required to match. See the notes on page 46.

The finished basket-weave seat has a comfortable and casual look.

ALTERNATE METHOD FOR BASKET WEAVE ON A SEAT WITH SLOPING SIDE RAILS

For a seat with sloping side rails and the warp running from front to back, the warp pairs are splayed to fit by adding wrappings on the front rail. You can be super-exacting, by dividing the back and front rails into seven or nine segments as desired, or throw caution to the winds, and simply mark centers on the front and back rails. The latter works fine.

Begin by bringing the tie end below the back rail and nailing it to the inner left rail. Bring the weaving end forward over the front rail, snug to both left posts. Go back across the underside, around the back rail, and across the top again to form the first warp pair. On the front rail, make three wraps (figure 5.13). Bring the weaver across the bottom, under the back rail snug to the previous cane, and make two wraps (figure 5.14). Now it's on top, ready to do another pair.

Note that this pair of warps is parallel to the sloping side rail. But because you are making three wraps on the front rail and only two wraps on the back rail, the warp pairs will eventually line up parallel to each other and at right angles to the front rail. Continue wrapping with three spacers in front and two in back until the warps are at right angles to the front rail, which will happen somewhere toward the center of the seat. The center pair should come close to being on the center marks. Alternatively,

you could wrap the front with three, then two. Beyond the center marks, work to correspond with the left half.

As you are wrapping this warp, make joins on the inside of the front or back rail as shown in figures 5.10 and 5.11. Be careful to catch the tie end of the new cane in the previous wrap to hold it securely.

End with a pair of warps against the right front post, with one cane width empty next to the rear post. Bring the weaver across the bottom, up around the back rail next to the post, down in front of the corner post, below the right rail, and up to the top so that it is ready to weave right to left as the first strand of weft.

Weave over the first pair, under the next, and so on across to the left rail. With your fingers, push this strand tight against the back posts and straight across. Bring the weaving end around the left rail, turn the chair upside down, and weave across the underside in the same way, traveling over one pair and under the next. Turn the chair upright and weave the second weft on the top, this time going under where the first strand went over. Continue until you reach the center of the side rails.

At the midpoint change on the underside (figure 5.12), start weaving the warp pairs on the underside as they are divided into pairs on the front rail. Weave the seat to the front posts.

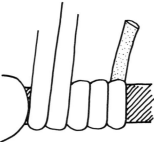

5.13 For a seat with sloping side rails, form the first warp pair, then make three wraps on the front rail.

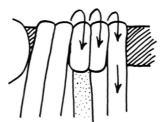

5.14 Bring the weaver across the bottom, under the back rail snug to the previous cane, and make two wraps.

DANISH ROPE

CHAPTER VI

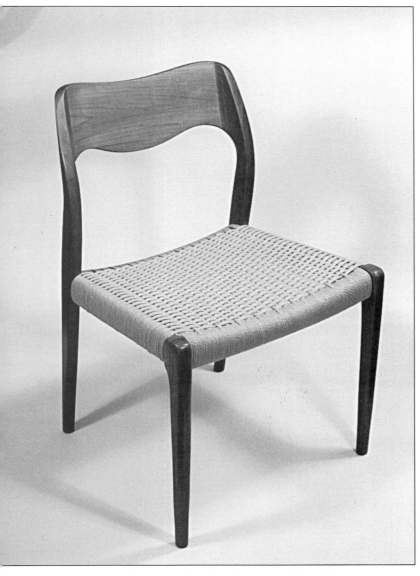

A Danish rope chair with single side rails. Courtesy of Carol Buxton.

Tools and Materials
A Single-Rail Chair Seat
Variations
   Double rails
   Flat rails
Double Rail—Cane

Teakwood chairs with clean, sculptured lines and handwoven rope seats have been widely popular since World War II. Originating in Denmark and Sweden, they are of two major types, those with solid rails on all four sides and those with split double rails on the right and left sides. Some styles have beech or oak frames, and many have beech rails set in a teak frame.

The rope used to weave the seats of these chairs is firmly twisted three-strand paper rope, about 1/8 inch in diameter. This Danish rope differs from imitation rush rope in its finer size, texture, and quality. It is available in one color, golden brown, and in two formats: laced, in which the twists are prominent, and unlaced, with smoother twists. The latter is the type most commonly used. In all cases, the rope is woven dry.

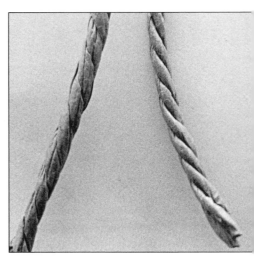

Danish rope is available as unlaced (left) and laced (right).

TOOLS AND MATERIALS

You'll need about two pounds of paper rope for each chair seat, side-cutting pliers or tin snips, 1/2-inch flathead nails, a hammer, scissors, and a screwdriver. Many L-shaped nails hold the rope in place on the underside of the chair; should you break off any of them as you remove the old seat, you'll need replacements (see Suppliers).

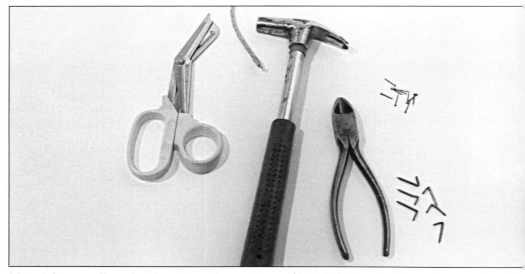

Materials you will need: side-cutting pliers, scissors, 1/2-inch flathead nails, replacement L nails as necessary, two pounds of paper rope per chair, a hammer. You'll also need a screwdriver and awl for coaxing the weft through tight places.

WEAVING A SINGLE-RAIL CHAIR SEAT

Preparation

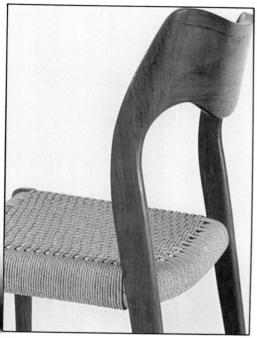

This single-rail Danish chair has four solid rails with spaced doubled warps and closely woven double wefts.

Before cutting off the old seat, make notes of its pattern so that you can duplicate the weaving in the new seat. Usually there are four vertical strands (warps) on the extreme right and left sides; otherwise, the warps are paired. In most cases, you'll find an odd number of warp pairs. Note that all four rails are wrapped with rope between the warps and wefts (horizontals). The front rail is wrapped as the warp is applied to the chair; the back rail, after the warp is wound; and the side rails, along with the weaving.

Cut off the old seat from the top with heavy side-cutting pliers or tin snips. Short pieces of rope will still be held in place by the L-shaped nails on the inside of the rails. Use side-cutting pliers to grab the shank of each nail and pry it up from the edge $1/16$ to $1/8$ inch (figure 6.1). Do not remove the nails, as you will use them again. Avoid pulling up on the tip of the nail, as it may break. Remove all of the rope loops from the nails.

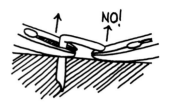

6.1 Pry up the L-shaped nails with side-cutting pliers.

Cut the old seat off the chair with scissors. Loops will remain hanging from the nails on the rails.

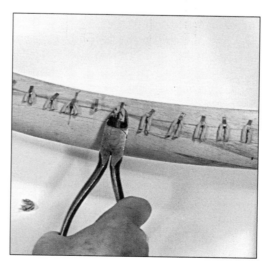

With side-cutting pliers, pry up the nails from the sides $1/16$ to $1/8$ inch. Remove the rope loops. Be careful not to break off the nails, as you will reuse them.

6.2 Loop the end of the rope around the corner L nail.

Warping

The first step is to wrap the warp between the front and back of the seat. Cut off a length of rope 10 to 12 yards long. The length of the working rope is not critical—the shorter the length, the more joins; the longer the length, the more tangles you'll encounter as you wrap. I've found a rope length of about 10 yards to be a happy medium.

Either nail the starting end on the front rail close to the left corner with two ¹/₂-inch flat-head nails, or loop the rope on the L nail at the corner by folding the end of the rope over the nail and winding over the loop with the working end to lock it in place (figure 6.2).

Cut off 10 to 12 yards of rope and loop one end over the corner nail on the left front. Hold the short end of the loop down as you pull the long end of the rope over it to the lower inside, then up, around, and over the front rail.

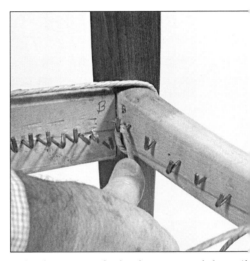

Take the rope to the back, go around the nail in the corner, then up and over the back rail and back to the front.

❖ In most cases, I've specified working right to left or left to right, but you may work in the opposite directions if you so desire.

Wrap the rope around the first nail again. Come up and around as before and return to the back, wrapping around the same nail.

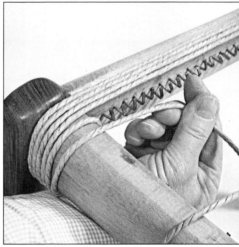

Wrap the front rail until you reach the next nail. You now have four warp ends lying side by side.

To begin weaving, bring the rope under the front rail, around the outside, and then up over the top. Take it over and around the back rail and hook it on the first left-hand nail on the back rail. To begin the second warp, bring the rope down, around the outside of the back rail, and then over the top and back to the front. Go over the top of the front rail and up on the inside to hook the rope again on the rail where you began. You now have two strands lying next to each other. Repeat by bringing the rope down from the L nail, up around the outside of the front rail, to the back, then over and around the back rail to the same L nail you wrapped around the last pass. Hook the rope on this nail and return to the front. You now have four warps lying side by side.

For spacers between warps, wrap four or five turns around the front rail, crowding the wraps together, until the rope touches the next nail to the right. On the next wrap, bring the rope up over the top and carry it to the back rail. Hook the rope around the second nail, and return to the front rail and hook the rope around the second nail. You'll now have two warps lying next to each other. Wrap around the front rail until you reach the next hook (it is not necessary that each space have the same number of wraps; just fill the space

neatly). Repeat, winding paired warps and wrapping the front rail between nails until you reach the last hook, when you will wind four warps together as you did on the other side.

When you run out of rope, make the join on the front rail by looping the end of the old piece over a nail, then beginning the new piece with a loop that holds down the tails of both the old and new pieces (figure 6.3).

It is desirable to have 3 to 4 yards of rope left over after the last warp has been wound for starting the weft. Take the rope from the last hook at the right side of the front rail under the right side rail and around the outside to the top. Slide your fingers along the rope for about 18 inches and fold it into a loop. This removes some of the twist from the rope and gives you a looped end to work for the weft. Weave this loop over the four warps at the right edge, then under the next pair of warps. Pull taut and stop. This will hold the weaver in place until you are ready to continue with it.

Turn the chair over and pound down the nails on the front and back rails. While the chair is upside down, attach one end of a 6-yard-long piece of rope for wrapping the back rail to the right corner of the back rail.

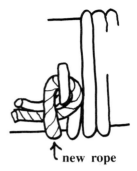

6.3 Begin a new length of rope by looping it over the ending loop.

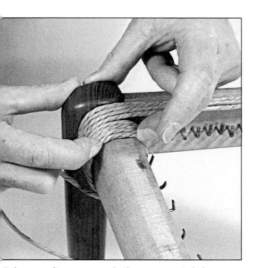

With your fingers, push the wraps tightly together.

On the final filler wrap, come up and around the front and carry the rope over the top to the back rail.

❖ Keep a constant medium tension so that the ropes lie straight and even. The warps will tighten as the weft is woven.

Go over the top, around the back, and hook the rope over the second nail. Come back up and around the outside, over the top, and back to the front. You'll now have two warps lying next to each other.

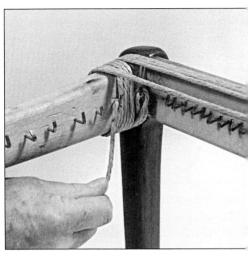

Wrap around the nail on the front rail as you did in back and wrap the front rail to the next nail.

When you run out of rope, loop the end of a new rope length over the old loop on the same nail.

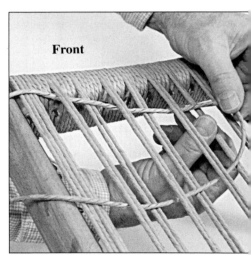

Wind the final four warps and then bring the weaver up and around the side rail and weave it through a few warps to hold it in place until you are ready to start weaving.

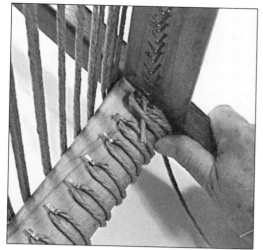

Cut a length of rope 10 to 15 yards long. Turn the chair over and either nail the rope end or loop the end over the last corner nail.

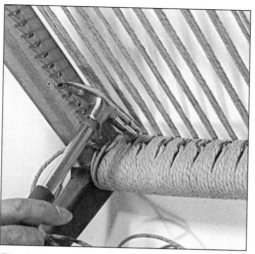

Firmly hammer in all the nails at front and back.

Wrapping the back rail

Turn the chair upright and wrap this rope tightly around the back rail to fill the spaces between the warp pairs. Crowd the spaces as you did for the front rail, being sure that the rope lies flat and smooth on the bottom, outside, and top of the back rail. Any time the rope crosses another one, it should do so on the inside of the rail. If you run out of rope, nail on another length on the inside of the rail (figure 6.4). To finish, nail the end of the rope to the inside left corner of the back rail.

Wrap the back rail to fill in the spaces between the warp. Cross ropes only on the inside. Use the hammer as necessary to pound the rope or nails into place. Secure the ends with nails at the other corner.

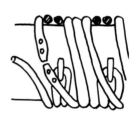

6.4 Wrapping the back rail. To begin a new rope, nail the old and new ends to the inside of the rail.

Weaving the weft

Pick up the weaver you left waiting at the right front corner. Continue weaving the loop across, over one pair of warps, under the next pair, and so on. Let the tail slide along behind. In this way, you can weave two wefts following the same path at the same time. When you reach the left side of the chair, weave over the four edge warps. Straighten the first weft against the front rail. Then pull the loop 6 inches beyond the rail, underneath on the left, and pull the rope reasonably tight as you hook it over the L-shaped nail on the inside of the side rail. Straighten and snug up this second rope against the first. Hook the rope on the next nail on the right rail.

Slide your fingers out about 18 inches to make the next loop and repeat for the next pass of weft, taking the next loop *under* the first four warps and over the next pair, following the opposite path of the first two wefts. Continue to weave in this way until the side rails are full. As your weaving will probably pack in tighter than the distance between the nails, you'll need to double up some rows on the hooks.

When you need to start a new piece of rope, nail the old end to the inside of the right side rail and cut it short. Cut an 8- to 10-yard length of rope from the roll and run it through your fingers at least twice to get the kinks out and relax it before weaving. Nail one end of it over the top of the piece you just ended, and continue the weaving. You also may be able to make a new join as shown in figure 6.3.

On the last weft pair, the space will be very tight; you'll need to weave with a single rope end rather than a loop, but maintain the same paired-weft pattern. Nail the end to the inside of the right side rail and cut it short.

Fillers

If the back of the seat curves outward, a row or two of filler wefts may be needed to close the gap. Nail individual pieces of rope to the inside of the back rail and weave back and forth as necessary (figure 6.5).

Finish the job by pounding in the L nails on the sides.

top

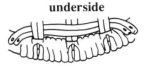

underside

6.5 If the chair seat has a curved back, weave filler wefts to close up the space. Nail pairs of rope to the inside rail and weave back and forth as needed.

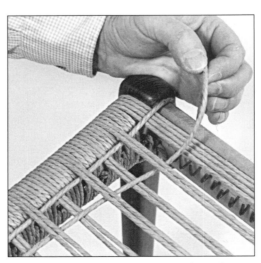

With a loop from the tail left over from the warp, weave to the other side and hook the loop on the first nail on the side rail.

Straighten first one weft and then the next, cramming them together with your fingers. Hook the loop on the nail the ends on the inside of the rail.

Bottom view of the finished chair.

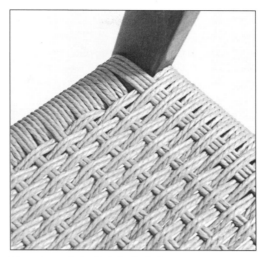

Top view of the finished chair.

VARIATIONS
Double rails

Some Danish chairs have divided side rails (double rails) with no L nails and solid rails with nails at the front and back. On these chairs, warp the chair seat as described above, except cut off the end of the rope when you finish warping and nail the end to the inside of the rail. Wrap the back rail as before.

To begin weaving the weft, cut off 15 to 20 yards of rope and run it through your fingers to relax it. Nail the two cut ends to the in-side front corner of the right rail. Take both ropes under the bottom rail and around the outside of both rails, and over the top, keeping them parallel and untwisted (figure 6.6). Weave across, over the first four warps and under the next two warps. Wrap around both rails on the left, bringing the pair up on the inside, then *BETWEEN* the rails to the outside. Wrap the bottom rail once. Again, bring the pair *BETWEEN* the rails to the outside (figure 6.7A). Now, bring the rope around on top

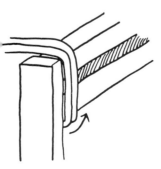

6.6 Wrapping the right side of a double-rail chair seat.

of the upper rail and weave across to the other side. Go over the right rail, then between the rails to the inside, then around the bottom rail to the inside again, come out on the outside at the bottom, come up over both rails to begin weaving the next row (figure 6.7B). Weave back to the other side. After a few rounds, your pattern will look like figure 6.8.

For the first three-quarters of the seat, you can use a loop to weave (figure 6.9). The last few wefts at the back will have to be woven with a single strand. If you need to make a join, nail the old and new ends on the inside of a lower side rail (figure 6.10). Weft filler rows may be needed at the back; if so, add them as described above for the chair with solid rails.

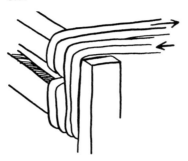

6.7A Wrapping the left side of a double-rail chair seat.

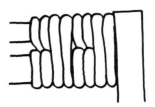

6.8 After several rounds, the sides of a double-rail seat look like this.

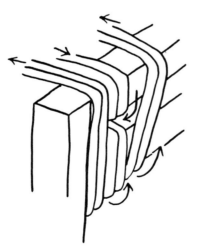

6.7B Wrapping the right, second time.

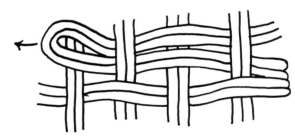

6.9 Weave the first three-quarters of the seat with a loop.

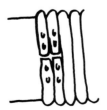

6.10 Join the old and new ends by nailing them to the inside of the lower rail.

lat rails on all four sides

Some Danish side chairs have wide (about -inch) flat rails on all four sides. On all the hairs of this style that I've seen, the side ils are worked a little differently from the receding instructions. You'll probably find at the rope on the old seat was attached to the inside rails with tacks or nails. Remove these completely when you remove the old eat. When winding the new warp, you'll eed to tack it on the inside rails, instead of hooking it over L nails. Wind paired warps, spaced apart, as described for the chairs above.

Instead of using doubled wefts as in the first two examples, weave the weft singly over the warp pairs (look carefully at the original rope before you cut it off and then duplicate its pattern) and then wrap around once on the side rails before weaving over to the other side (figure 6.11).

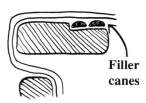

Nail

Warps

6.11 An alternative method is to weave the weft singly over the warp pairs and then wrap around the side rails once before weaving over to the other side.

DOUBLE-RAIL CHAIR WOVEN WITH 5 MM CANE

Sometimes you may find a Hans Wegner hair with double rails closely woven with 5 m cane instead of Danish rope. Except for me additional preparation and the different haracteristics of cane as opposed to Danish pe, the technique is essentially that described for the double-rail chair above. The op and sides of this hybrid are shown in fig- re 6.12.

First cut out the center of the seat as close the rails as possible. Nailed to the inside of the front and back rails will be half-round rat-n strips, forming a decorative cover to hide row of small flathead nails. With a ³/₄-inch hisel, carefully lift the strips so that the at-ching nails begin to come out. Finish pull-ng them out with side-cutting pliers, taking pains not to split the cane. These strips will be reinstalled in their original positions at the finish. Lay them aside for now.

Unwrap the cane from the side rails and pull it away from the flathead nails on the front and back rails. This leaves the nailheads slightly elevated from the wood surface so that you can use the side-cutting pliers to pull them out completely.

You'll notice now that the cane has been cut away. The inner top edge has two pieces of cane (called filler canes) placed along this length (figure 6.13). The cane loops through a hole at each corner juncture (figure 6.14). Remove these filler canes. If you have not already done so, put the replacement cane in to soak.

Filler canes

6.13 Cane used as padding.

top view

side view

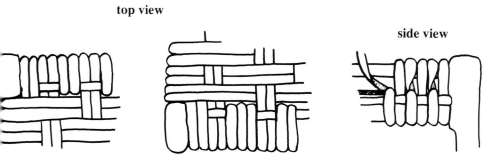

.12 A chair with double rails closely woven with 5 mm cane is woven like a double-rail hair of Danish rope.

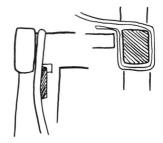

6.14 To put a new filler cane on the side rail, bring one end up through the hole at the back of one side. Leave a 1-inch tail lying flat on the rail where the longer length of cane will cover it. Bring the long end of the cane around the back rail, over the top, and to the front rail. Secure the end of the filler cane under the top cane in front by taking the tail of the filler cane around the front rail and up through the hole. Pull it tight, trim to 1 inch, then bend this stub down flat and slip it under the top cane.

Look for pencil lines along the center of the lower side rails and a line with tick marks on the front and back rails. Nails should be placed along the lines; the tick marks on the front and back rails mark the placement for the warp pairs.

Begin by putting in new pairs of filler canes on the left and right rails. Bring one end up through the hole at the back of one side. Leave a 1-inch tail lying flat on the rail where the longer length of cane will cover it (figure 6.14). Bring the long end of the cane around the back rail, over the top, and to the front rail. Cut it off about 6 inches beyond the rail. Take this tail around the front rail and up through the hole. Pull it tight, trim to 1 inch, and bend this stub down flat. Slip it under the top cane (figure 6.14). No nails are needed for this procedure because the pressure of the cane on top will hold everything in place. Repeat with the other three filler canes so that there are two on each side rail.

Next, install the warps, starting on the inside back rail (figure 6.15). Lay the chair on its back with the legs pointing toward you. Make a neat square cut on the cane end with small side-cutting pliers, and position this end even with the top inside edge of the rail. If you start in the left corner and work right, the first cane will lie to the left of the first vertical tick on the pencil line. Fasten this cane with a ½-inch nail. Pull the length of cane around the back rail and up over the top to the front rail. Wrap it around the front rail to judge the length and cut to end at the top of the inner front rail. Let the end hang loose for now. Go to the back rail and nail the second cane alongside the first (figure 6.16) and cut this second warp to the same length as the first warp. Nail all pairs across the back rail in the same way, placing each pair on either side of a tick mark.

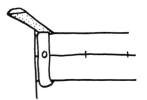

6.15 Position the square-cut end even with the top inside edge of the back rail with its edge lined up with the first vertical tick on the pencil line. Fasten this cane with a ½-inch nail.

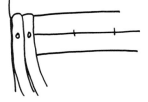

6.16 Nail the second cane alongside the first on the other side of the tick mark.

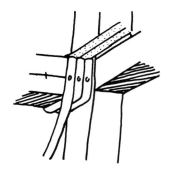

6.17 Nail a long cane on the inner back rail to start the wraps that will fill in between the warps. Do the same on the front rail.

To nail all the canes on the front rail, turn the chair over so that the front rail is flat on the table, with the legs still pointing to you. Starting at the left side, take the first cane over the back rail, across the seat, and around the front rail. Hold the end of the cane flat against the inside left corner of the front rail, to the left of the first tick mark. Nail the cane on the horizontal pencil line. If necessary trim the tail if it is not flush with the top inside edge. Keep the tension medium, only so the canes lie flat. Continue across the front rail until all warp pairs have been nailed.

Next, you must wrap the back and front rails to fill in the spaces between the warp pairs while adding a trim piece of cane. Nail a fresh length of cane to the inside right corner of the back rail (figure 6.17). Then find a short length of 5 mm cane that is longer than the rail from post to post. Insert the end of this piece of cane under the two filler canes on the right end of the top of the rail, position-ing it near the inner edge of the rail (figure 6.18). This trim piece will go over the warps but under the wrap that you are about to do, giving it a woven appearance. Now wrap the rail with the longer piece, always wrapping over the trim piece. Crowd the canes snugly together as you wrap. Cross over to the next space at an angle on the inside of the rail (fig-ure 6.19). Add new lengths as needed (figure 6.20).

When you finish wrapping, nail the end of the wrapping cane to the inside of the back rail on the horizontal pencil line. Cut the left end of the trim piece flush with the post and slip the end under the two filler canes on the left (figure 6.21). Repeat for the front rail. Be-cause there's more space between warps, you may need to make more wraps on the front than the back.

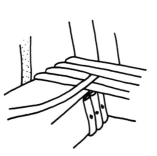

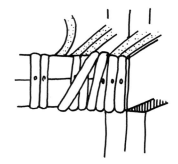

6.18 Insert the end of a trim piece under two filler canes on the right end of the top of the rail, near the inner edge. The trim will go over the warps but under the wrap, giving it a woven appearance.

6.19 Nail a fresh cane to the inside right corner of the back rail. Cross over to the next space at an angle on the inside of the rail.

6.20 Add new lengths as needed by overlapping the new and old canes and securing the ends with a nail on the pencil line.

6.21 When you finish wrapping, cut the left end of the trim piece flush with the post and slip it under the two filler canes on the left.

Start the weft by nailing the end of a long length of cane to the inside of the lower right side rail, snug to the front corner. (You can start at either side, whichever is more comfortable.) Unlike with the double-rail chairs woven with rope, you'll weave with a single weft instead of a doubled one. Bring the weaving end around the two side rails to the top. Weave over the first four canes, then under two, over two to the left side, where the weft goes over the four warps. Pull the cane tight and crowd it to the front. Go around both rails and come out between them (figure 6.22A), then around the lower rail and out between them again (figure 6.22B). Pull the cane taut and twist it at the point where it touches the top rail so that the shiny side is up (figure 6.22C).

Keep this side wrap tight by holding the cane in position against the wood with your left hand as you weave two stitches to the right and then pull the cane through. This holds the twist in place. Weave back to the other side, following the same path as the first weft. This completes the first matched pair of wefts.

Before starting the next weft, choose two lengths of 5 mm cane 2 inches longer than the side rails to serve as trim pieces on the outside of the lower side rails. These must be positioned before any more weaving is done. With an awl, slip the end of the trim under the first wrap at the front end of the lower left side rail, bend back $1/4$ inch of the end of the trim piece, and slide the bent portion under the first weft cane (figure 6.23). Do the same on the right. These trim pieces may not stay

in place at first, but we will fix them pronto as more wefts are woven. On the right, take the weaver between the two side rails, pull tight, and twist it so that the shiny side is out as it goes over the inside of the lower rail (figure 6.24A). Holding the trim in place, wrap the weaver over it, then take the weaver between the rails (figure 6.24B). Bring it out below the lower rail and under the trim piece (figure 6.24C).

Now weave across the seat, following the opposite path to that of the first pair of wefts. On the left, the weaver goes straight down, under the trim, wraps once around the lower rail over the trim, comes out between the rails, twists, and is ready for the next weft. Make all the twists in the same direction. Now the weaver follows the previous weft to make a pair. Continue weaving to the back of the seat.

When the length of cane is used up, make joins on the inside of the lower rail, keeping the nails used to make each join lined up on the horizontal pencil line (figure 6.25). Crowd the wraps on the left and right rails together often so that there are no gaps. Nail the last weft tail on the inside rail face on either the left or right rail.

Cut the trim piece on each lower side rail $1/4$ inch beyond the last weft and tuck it in (figure 6.26). Replace the rattan half-rounds in their original positions on the inside of the front and back rails over the rows of nailheads. Secure with $1/2$-inch nails. A finish on the cane is not needed, but buffing with wax will do no harm.

6.22 Go around both rails and come out between them (A), then around the lower rail and out between them again (B). Pull the cane taut and twist it at the point where it touches the top rail so that the shiny side is out (C).

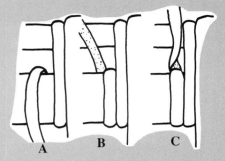

6.23 With an awl, slip the end of the trim under the first wrap at the front end of the lower left side rail (A); then bend back ¹/₄ inch of the end of the trim piece and slide it under the first weft cane (B).

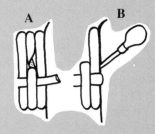

6.24 On the right, take the weaver between the two side rails, pull tight, and twist it so that the shiny side is out as it goes over the inside of the lower rail (A). Holding the trim in place, wrap the weaver over it, then take the weaver between the rails (B). Bring it out below the lower rail and under the trim piece (C).

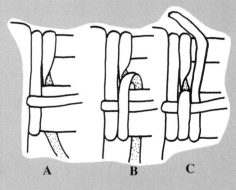

6.25 Make joins on the inside of the lower rail by lapping the new end over the old. Keep the nails lined up on the horizontal pencil line.

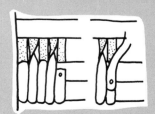

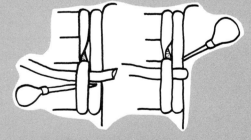

6.26 To end the trim piece on the lower side rail, cut it ¹/₄ inch beyond the last weft and tuck it in as you did at the other end.

DIVIDING A RAIL INTO EQUAL SEGMENTS

On a chair on which a front or back rail has been replaced with new wood or a layout for this pattern has not previously been made, you'll need to make the pencil lines and tick marks for the warps yourself before beginning to weave. The warp pairs must be an uneven number, say five.

Rather than measure each rail and then figure out how many inches to allow between each mark, try this method for the layout. Take a piece of paper wide enough to cover the distance between the inner faces of the side rails on the back rail plus at least $1/2$ inch. Draw a line near the lower edge of this paper and on that line mark the width of the back rail, leaving at least a $1/4$-inch margin of paper beyond the marks. Draw a pencil line at about a 30-degree angle to the base line, starting at the farthest left mark (figure 6.27). Mark this new line every 2 inches or so (the exact distance doesn't matter, so long as the marks are evenly spaced) until you have five segments. Connect the last tick on the upper line to the mark on the base line at the lower right which represents the right end of the back rail, making a triangle. Draw lines from the top points to the bottom line; a wide ruler and your eye will help you make the lines parallel. These lines will intersect the bottom line to divide it into five equal segments.

Now cut your paper so that you have a long strip that includes the lower line plus $1/4$ inch at either end. Tape this strip to the inside of the back seat rail, matching the end marks to the corners and bending the paper to match the curve. Push an awl through the paper to mark the wood at the points. Remove the paper strip.

If the front rail also needs to be marked, repeat the above process with a new piece of paper, as the front rail is longer than the back.

This technique can be used whenever you need to divide a length into equal segments.

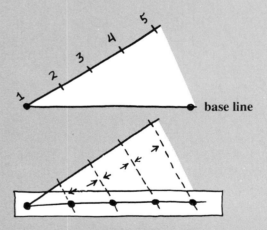

6.27 Dividing a line into equal segments.

REPAIRS

CHAPTER VII
FIXING A HAND-CANED BENTWOOD FRAME

Few pieces of furniture, antiques in particular, make it through life without requiring some kind of repair. Caning is not an isolated job: the supporting structure must be made sound before caning can begin.

The correct sequence in dealing with any chair is to strip, glue, finish, then cane. Caning before finishing makes for unnecessary work in masking out the cane during finishing. Don't cane a chair with joints so loose it resembles a folding chair; glue it first. Don't fall for "joint tightener"—glycerin that you inject with a syringe into the loose joint. The glycerin causes the wood to absorb water from the air to achieve an impermanent and dubious "fix". Loud squeaks are a by-product.

Some stripping (paint-removing) processes are death to glue. For a fine piece, nothing beats complete dismantling, stripping the individual parts by hand, and then sanding and regluing. It takes time, is costly, and is worth it.

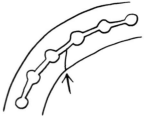

7.1 For splits in a hand-caned bentwood frame, use a fine coping saw to make an angling cut on the inner frame, avoiding the cane holes.

Fixing Splits Down a Row of Holes

Peculiar to hand caning are unfortunate splits right down the row of holes. Reattaching the broken piece with nails or dowels, as many have done, is inadequate; it will eventually let go again. The glue of choice in the following instances is Titebond® or Elmer's Carpenter's Wood Glue®. If the entire length is split, apply the glue to the areas between holes and clamp. When dry, put in four flat-head wood screws, set exactly between the cane holes. A special stair-stepped drill with built-in countersink is handy for this. Use #6 by 1¼-inch screws so that they do not come out on the other side of the frame. To repair a partial split, work the glue into the cracks with a short piece of Fine cane. Clamp. When dry, drill and put in screws. Clean the glue out of the cane holes with the proper size drill.

7.2 Drill holes for two screws on each side of the cut, glue, and put in screws. Slide a glued veneer piece or pieces into the saw cut. Clamp right over the screws. When dry, remove clamps, tighten screws, shave off the surplus veneer, sand, and drill the glue out of the cane holes.

Fixing Splits in a Hand-caned Bentwood Frame

For splits in a hand-caned bentwood frame, a round or oval back for instance, use a fine coping saw to make an angling cut on the inner frame, avoiding the cane holes (figure 7.1). Drill holes for two screws on each side of the cut, glue, and put in screws (figure 7.2). Slide a glued veneer piece or pieces into the saw cut. Clamp right over the screws. When dry, remove clamps, tighten screws, shave off the surplus veneer, sand, and drill the glue out of the cane holes. An outside curve on bentwood with serious damage or splits is cut out with long sloping cuts at both ends (figure 7.3). Fill the gap with layers of veneer (maple is preferred) stair-stepped to fit the sloping ends and overhanging the circumference of the bentwood frame. Glue and clamp. When dry, shave the veneer down to size, finish with a fine file, sand, redrill the holes, and recarve the back groove if there is one. This type of lamination gives maximum strength and adapts well to a curve.

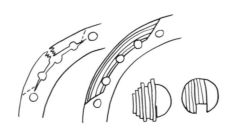

7.3 An outside curve on bentwood with serious damage or splits is cut out with long sloping cuts at both ends. Fill the gap with layers of veneer, stair-stepped to fit the sloping ends and overhanging the circumference of the bentwood stick. Glue and clamp. When dry, shave the veneer down to size, finish with a fine file, sand, redrill the holes, and recarve the back groove if there is one.

Fixing the Front Rail Of an Egg-Shaped Seat

The front curved rail of a walnut chair or rocker with an egg-shaped seat is prone to split over the front legs due to the grain direction in that area. If the whole chair is wobbly, all of the chair should be glued, but for now we will concentrate on the seat frame. Remove the frame from the chair and carefully knock apart the four rails. Reglue the split(s) on the front rail, first anchoring the pieces together with a brad to keep them from sliding (figure 7.4). When dry, check the dowels and replace the broken ones. Glue and clamp the four rails back together. To further strengthen the leg corners, add a kidney-bean reinforce-

ment. Sand the area behind the leg holes to remove varnish, glue, and dirt. Glue a ⅛-inch-thick "bean" made of walnut or mahogany to the frame (figure 7.5). When dry, redrill the holes from the top, and bevel the edges of the bean with a sharp chisel. Another way to strengthen the corners is to put a long "knee" in each corner (figure 7.6). In severe cases use both the knee and the bean to ensure that the frame will support the cane and will not collapse when sat on. The wood of choice for the above repairs is mahogany. It has a firm, strong, but not hard grain, is easily shaped, and is stable, not hygroscopic like pine.

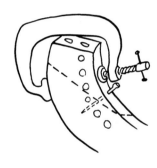

7.4 To repair a split in a front curved rail, remove the frame from the chair and carefully knock apart the four rails. Reglue the split(s) on the front rail by anchoring with a brad to keep the pieces from sliding.

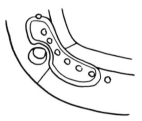

7.5 To further strengthen the leg corners, glue a ⅛-inch-thick "bean" made of walnut or mahogany to the frame.

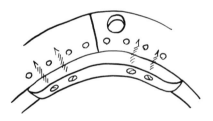

7.6 Another way to strengthen the corners is to put a long "knee" in each corner.

Replacing a Broken Rail

To replace a broken seat rail on a chair made for rush or splint, the front legs and stretchers are separated from the back posts, the rail is reproduced and fitted, and the whole front assembly reglued and then glued to the back posts (see Anatomy of a Chair on page 11). If the original rail was handmade or not, ours will be handmade. Trace it on new stock. Bandsaw or chop with a hatchet to the rough outline. Shape further with a chisel, and make round tenons on each end with a coarse rasp. When the tenon nearly fits the hole, change to a medium file to make a final tight fit. In gluing a front leg assembly, try to keep it intact before gluing. Knock the right front leg away from the front stretchers, apply a generous bead of glue to the holes, not the tenons. Pound the tenons back into holes. Then knock the left front leg away from the front stretchers, glue, and pound these tenons back in immediately. Then do the side stretchers one at a time. Be sure that the stretchers go back into the holes in their original positions, without being turned and without reversing the tenons. After the new rail has been installed and the front assembly glued to the back posts, use a bar clamp to tighten the tenons successively on all four sides. Then tighten a band clamp or two around the legs until the glue is set.

To make tenons on a dowel used for a rung, use the coping saw to cut around it, the length of the tenon from each end (figure 7.7). With the ³/₄-inch chisel, split off thin slices from the end to make rough, oversize tenons (figure 7.8). Round them with the rasp, and then use a fine file to fit (figure 7.9). This method gets results with simple tools in a short time and bypasses a tenon cutter or a lathe, neither of which may be in your tool collection.

When it is not desirable or possible to separate the front parts from the back posts, saw the broken rail in two and remove it, keeping the major parts. If the tenon has broken off at the post, drill a good-sized hole in the center of it and chisel out the remainder. Trace and make a new rail as in the preceding paragraph, allowing for any broken tenons. Saw

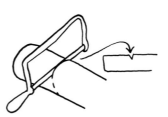

7.7 To make a tenon on a dowel used for a rung, use the coping saw to cut around it, the length of the tenon from the end.

the new rail in two in a long sloping cut with the finest saw available (figure 7.10). A Dremel jigsaw (a small electric jigsaw with a very fine blade, which removes minimal wood) does an excellent job. Try tenons for size in the post holes. File for a snug fit. Glue tenons and insert. Glue the saw cut and clamp. A dowel used as a rung is treated in the same manner. Further strengthening (as for a wide cane seat in twill) can be done by filing a flat on the inner side of the dowel after installation, and gluing and clamping a ¹/₈-inch batten to it. When dry, shave the corners off the batten with the chisel. The result is a very sturdy rail, probably stronger than the original.

A component of Lincoln rockers that is cause for concern is a strip of wood on each side of the back posts. ("Lincoln" applies very loosely to tall-back rockers from the last half of the nineteenth century with hand-caned seat and back.) The strip of wood was drilled for cane and fastened to the post with square nails. These invariably pull out due to the cane's stress on them. While the cane is out, these strips must be reglued and refastened with wood screws. If the screw heads offend, countersink and putty them. The square-cut, machine-made nails are no great shakes as antiques. Hand-wrought square iron nails come from much earlier in the century and might be worth saving. You will have to tell me what for.

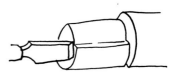

7.8 With the ³/₄-inch chisel split off thin slices from the end to make a rough, oversize tenon.

7.9 Round the tenon with the rasp, and then use a fine file to fit.

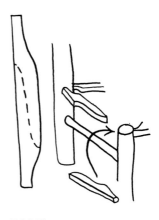

7.10 If you cannot separate the front legs from the back posts, saw the broken rail and remove it, keeping the major parts. Trace and make a new rail. Saw the new rail in two in a long, sloping cut with a fine saw. Glue the two halves to the posts, then glue the saw cut and clamp.

EPILOGUE

To the many customers who have entrusted their chairs to me over the years and who have made possible all the experiences recounted here, I give my warmest thanks. May the techniques I have described guide the beginning and accomplished caner to a successful completion of his or her project. The best advice to this end is to keep an open mind. My encouragement and best wishes go with you.

George Sterns, Denver, Colorado, 1990.

SUPPLIERS

Cane & Basket Supply Co.
1283 S. Cochran
Los Angeles, CA 90019
(213) 939-9644
Hand and machine cane; imitation and natural rush; flat reed, ash, and paper splint; Danish rope; Shaker tape

The Caning Shop
926 Gilman Street
Berkeley, CA 94710
(415) 527-5010
Hand and machine cane; imitation rush; flat reed; rattan splint; rawhide; ash and paper splint; Shaker tape; Danish rope

Craftsman Wood Service Co.
1735 W. Cortland Ct.
Addison, IL 60101
(708) 629-3100
Wood; veneer; imitation rush; hand and machine cane

Frank's Cane & Rush
7252 Heil Ave.
Huntington Beach, CA 92647
(714) 847-0707
Hand and machine cane; imitation rush; Danish rope; rattan splint; wide cane

H.H. Perkins Co.
10 S. Bradley Road
Woodbridge, CT 06525
(203) 389-9501
Hand and machine cane; imitation and natural rush; paper and ash splint; wide cane; Shaker tape; Danish rope

Inter-Mares Trading Co.
Rte 109 Box 617
Lindenhurst, NY 11757
(516) 957-3467
Wholesale only: *hand and machine cane; imitation rush; rattan splint; sea grass*

Shaker Workshops
PO Box 1028
Concord, MA 01742-1028
(617) 646-8985
Cotton Shaker tape

Tole House Antiques
2711 S. Broadway
Englewood, CO 80110
(303) 761-4238
Hand and machine cane; imitation rush; hickory, oak, and ash splint; Danish rope; wide cane

Unfinished Universe
525 W. Short Street
Lexington, KY 40507
(606) 252-3289
Hickory and ash splint; hand and machine cane; imitation rush

Woodcraft
210 Wood County Industrial Park
PO Box 1686
Parkersburg, WV 26102
(800) 225-1153 to order
(800) 542-9115 for catalog
Tools, hand and machine cane; imitation rush

The Woodworkers' Store
21801 Industrial Blvd.
Rogers, MN 55374
(612) 428-2899
Wood; veneer; tools; hand and machine cane; imitation rush

CHAIR CANE SIZES, HOLE SIZES, AND HOLE SPACING

Size	Width mm	Hole diameter inches	Center to center inches (approx.)
Carriage	$1^1/_2$	$^1/_8$	$^5/_{16} - ^3/_8$
Superfine	$1^3/_4$	$^1/_8$	$^3/_8$
Fine-Fine	2	$^3/_{16}$	$^7/_{16} - ^1/_2$
Fine	$2^1/_2$	$^3/_{16}$	$^1/_2 - ^9/_{16}$
Narrow Med.	$2^3/_4$	$^{15}/_{64}$	$^9/_{16} - ^5/_8$
Medium	3	$^{15}/_{64} - ^1/_4$	$^5/_8 - ^{11}/_{16}$
Common	$3^1/_2$	$^5/_{16}$	$^3/_4 - ^7/_8$

SPLINE SIZES

Number	Width × Height mm	inches
$6^1/_2$	$2^1/_4 \times 3^3/_4$	$^3/_{32}$
7	3×5	$^7/_{64}$
$7^1/_2$	$3^1/_2 \times 5^1/_2$	$^9/_{64}$
8	$4 \times 5^1/_2$	$^5/_{32}$
$8^1/_2$	$4^1/_4 \times 6$	$^{11}/_{64}$
9	$4^3/_4 \times 6^1/_4$	$^3/_{16}$
$9^1/_2$	$5^1/_4 \times 7$	$^7/_{32}$
10	$5^3/_4 \times 7^1/_2$	$^{15}/_{64}$
$10^1/_2$	$6^1/_4 \times 8$	$^1/_4$
11	$6^3/_4 \times 8^3/_4$	$^{11}/_{64}$
12	$7^1/_2 \times 9^1/_2$	$^{19}/_{64}$

KINDS OF MACHINE CANE WEBBING

1-inch mesh

³/₄-inch mesh

⁵/₈-inch mesh

¹/₂-inch mesh

⁷/₁₆-inch mesh

³/₈-inch mesh

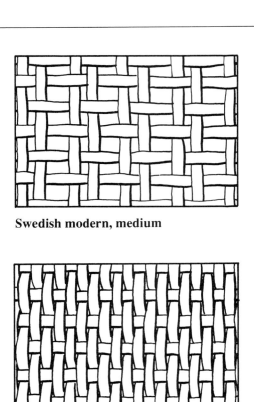

Swedish modern, medium

Swedish modern, fine

Close-woven, medium

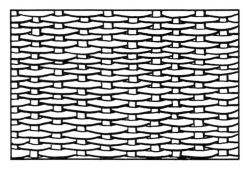

Close-woven, fine

Radio net, medium

Herringbone

Thanks to The Caning Shop for their assistance in preparing this chart.

Radio net, fine fine

Radio net, fine

HOW LONG WILL CANE, RUSH, SPLINT,
OR ROPE LAST?

How long will your tires last on your car? That depends. Heavy use, as in a restaurant, will shorten cane life drastically. You may be lucky to get a year out of it. The ubiquitous Breuer chair with a machine cane seat may hold up for five years. Here are some general figures based on long observation:

Hand cane–15 to 20 years
Imitation rush–20 to 50 years
Natural rush–50 to 75 years
Hickory splint–50 to 100 years
Machine cane–5 to 20 years
Paper splint–5 years
Danish rope–20 to 40 years

Appendix E

UNDERSTANDING WEAVE STRUCTURES

The simplest weave structure involves vertical elements (the warp) crossed at right angles by horizontal elements (the weft) in an over-one, under-one pattern called plain weave. In chair seat weaving, such as that seen on Shaker tape chairs, this is often called a checkerboard design. Plain weave is the strongest weave structure because it has the greatest number of intersections, but it is also the least flexible for the same reason.

Basket weave could be called a double plain weave because it has the same over-and-under pattern, but it is woven with paired warps and wefts. A variation of basket weave is half-basket weave, which is one set of paired elements, usually warps, crossed by a single element. An example of half-basket weave is the wide cane rocker shown in Chapter 5. Basket weave also encompasses any number of grouped elements crossing each other. For example, the bottom side of a wide cane chair seat might be woven in a three-over, three-under four-over, or four-under basket weave (see page 112). Because there are fewer intersections, a basket-weave chair seat will be more flexible.

Twills produce diagonal patterns. Moving over the interlacement one or more warps with each weft row offsets the pattern, which makes the diagonal line. Usually in chair seat weaving, you'll find 2/2 (two-over, two-under) and 3/3 twills (three-over, three under). In a 2/2 twill, for example, the weft will pass over two, under two in the first row. In the next row, to offset the weave, the weft will go over just one at the start and then follow the same over-two, under-two pattern. See the splint chair example in Chapter 4 for an example of a twill-woven chair seat.

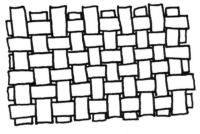

Plain weave

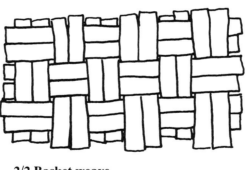

2/2 Basket weave

Half-basket weave

2/2 Twill

3/3 Twill

AWL–sharply pointed steel pick; bodkin

ASH–a hard wood that can be cut into long, thin strips for weaving a splint seat

BASKET WEAVE–a pattern of two or more adjacent strands woven in an over-under pattern

BENTWOOD–steam-bent frame with a continuous seat rail, either round or rectangular with rounded corners

BINDER–border strip of cane covering the holes in hand cane; usually wider than the cane in the center of seat; also called beading

BINDING–see binder

BLIND HOLE–hole that does not go through the frame

BULRUSH–plant with very tall leaves growing in swampy areas used for rush seats, *Scirpus lacustris*

BUTT–thick end of the rush leaf; the base

CANE–long strip cut from the inner bark of the rattan palm

CATTAIL–*Typha latifolia*

CHECKERBOARD–pattern created by weaving over one, under one; plain weave

CONCAVE SHAPE–curve that bulges inward

CONVEX SHAPE–curve that bulges outward

COUCHING–see lacing

DANISH ROPE–special paper rope about ¹/₈ inch in diameter; available as laced, in which the twists are more prominent, and unlaced, which has smoother twists

DEAD-BLOW HAMMER–nylon or rubber hammer with lead shot in the head to minimize bounce

DIAGONALS–in caning, the elements which are woven from bottom left to top right and top left to bottom right

DIVIDED CANES–pair of canes that go into separate holes rather than into a common hole; split cane

DOUBLE CANE–cane on two sides; on a chair back, one layer of weaving on the inside, and one layer of weaving on the outside

DOUBLE RAIL CHAIR SEAT–two rails, one above the other, often found on Danish chairs

FILLER–splint or cane woven along the edge to fill a gap

FILLER CANES–canes which act as a pad beneath the regular weaving

FISHHEAD–two diagonals that go into the same hole in hand caning

FLATHEAD NAIL–nail with a flat, round head, in contrast to a brad, which has only a knob for a head

FLAT RAILS–3- to 4-inch-wide by 1-inch-thick wood which makes up the four sides (rails) of a seat, joined by mortises or dowels

FRAME– the supporting structure of a cane seat, usually wood; the four rails

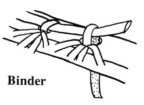

Binder

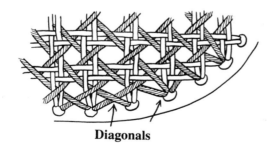

Diagonals

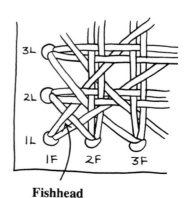

Fishhead

GUSSET–long triangle formed by sloping side rail that lies outside a rectangular layout

HALF-BASKET WEAVE–pattern in which pairs of elements cross single elements

HAND CANE–cane woven by hand into an octagonal pattern woven on chair seats or other furniture

HICKORY–wood split into long, thin strips used to weave chair seats

HORIZONTAL–weft in weaving; the direction in which the weaving material is woven

IMITATION RUSH–paper product twisted into rope to resemble natural rush

JOINT TIGHTENER–glycerin—not recommended

KNEE–wooden corner brace used to strengthen the corners of chair seats

LACING–finer cane woven through holes in the chair frame to hold the binder down; also called couching

LAYOUT–fixed points establishing the basis for a design

L NAIL–an L-shaped nail on which the rope is hooked in weaving on Danish chairs

MACHINE CANE–cane that is mechanically woven. It comes in a roll and can be cut off in seat-sized pieces, like yard goods

MORTISE–rectangular cavity into which a tenon fits, used to join seat rails or other chair parts

MULTIPLE WEAVERS–method of weaving wide cane with several wefts—not recommended

NATURAL RUSH–leaves of the bulrush or cattail plant twisted together to make a rope for weaving a rush seat

NODE–joint or bump on a plant stem where a leaf attaches

OAK–hard wood often shaved in long, thin strips for weaving a splint seat

PAPER SPLINT–thin, continuous strip manufactured to look like wood splint and used for chair seats; not very durable

PEGGED CANE–cane woven into blind holes

PLAIN WEAVE–over-one, under-one weave; the simplest weave structure

POST–long vertical member on either side of a chair back or front leg

RAIL–one of four members that constitute a seat frame

RELIEF CUTS–short cuts in the margin of machine cane that allow it to bend into the groove more easily

RUSH–(n.) bulrush or cattail leaves used for seat weaving, or paper imitation rope rush; (v.) to weave a seat by wrapping with rush in a particular pattern

SHAKER TAPE–cotton machine- or hand-woven material, $1/2$ to 1 inch wide, used to weave chair seats

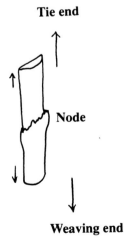

Tie end

Node

Weaving end

Relief cuts

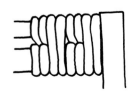

Double-rail chair seat

SIDE-CUTTING PLIERS–pointed pliers with two sharp cutting edges; also called wire-cutting pliers

SINGLE-RAIL CHAIR SEAT–a chair seat whose rails are each a single piece of wood

SLATS–horizontal back members, often curved; the "ladder" in a ladder-back chair

SLIP SEAT–seat frame that is independent of the chair frame, which usually sits down into a recess or on top of the frame

SLOT-AND-ARROW JOIN–method of joining hickory splint

SPLAT–thin, wide, vertical member in a chair back; sometimes pierced in a fancy design

SPLINE–rattan molding with rounded top and tapered sides used to anchor machine cane in a groove

SPLINT–flat wood strips for seat weaving

SPLIT CANES–pair of canes that go into separate holes rather than into one common hole; divided canes

STRETCHER–chair rung; the lower cross member bracing the legs, either a round dowel or a decorative turning.

STRIP–remove paint or varnish

STUFFING–cardboard or rush scraps used to fill the "pockets" in a rush seat

SUSPENDED MEDALLION–carved wood piece, often oval, in the center of a chair back that is supported by canes radiating from it to the outer chair back frame

TENON–a rectangular wood "tongue" that fits into a mortise

TIE END–the growing end of a cane strand, normally not the end you weave with

TIP–top of rush leaf; the thin end

THROUGH HOLE–hole that goes completely through the wood rail of a seat through which cane is woven

TWILL–pattern in which the weft shifts one or more warps to the left (or right) each row

V's–in hand caning, the V pattern at the edge that indicates that the diagonal interlacement has been woven incorrectly

VERTICAL–the warp, or the elements which run from the front of the chair to the back

WARP–The vertical elements of a woven chair seat, usually wrapped front to back

WEAVER–working end of the cane strand

WEAVING END–root end of the cane strand, normally the end used for weaving

WEFT–strand woven at right angles to the warp; a horizontal

WIDE CANE–4, 5, 6 mm cane that is usually woven in a twill pattern

WRAP–to wind cane or rope around the frame to cover or fill a space

X's–in hand caning, the X interlacement at the edge that indicates that the diagonals have been woven correctly

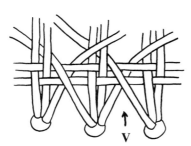

V

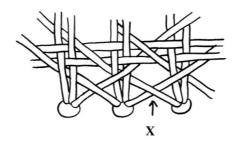

X

Bibliography

Alexander, John D. *Making a Chair From a Tree: An Introduction to Working Green Wood.* Newtown, CT: Taunton Press, 1978.

Bishop, Robert. *The American Chair.* New York: E.P. Dutton & Co., Inc., 1972.

Brazer, Esther Stevens. *Early American Decoration.* Springfield, MA: The Pond-Ekberg Company, 1961.

Brotherton, Germaine. *Rush and Leafcraft.* Boston: Houghton Mifflin Company, 1977.

Brown, Margery. *Cane and Rush Seating.* New York: Larousse and Co., Inc., 1976.

Comstock, Ruth B. *Rush Seats for Chairs.* Cornell Extension Bulletin 683. Ithaca, NY: Cornell University, 1968. Pamphlet.

—. *Splint Seats for Chairs.* Cornell Extension Bulletin 682. Ithaca, NY: Cornell University, 1967. Pamphlet.

Gloag, John. *The Chair.* New York: A.S. Barnes and Company, 1967.

Lea, Zilla Rider. *The Ornamented Chair.* Rutland, VT: Charles E. Tuttle Company, 1960.

Meador, Robert F.W. *Illustrated Guide to Shaker Furniture.* New York, New York: Dover Publications, Inc., 1972.

Miller, Bruce G., and Widess, Jim. *The Caner's Handbook.* New York: Van Nostrand Reinhold Co., 1983.

Miller, Edgar G., Jr. *American Antique Furniture.* New York, New York: Dover Publications, Inc. 1966.

Montgomery, Charles F. *American Furniture.* New York: Bonanza Books, 1978

Nutting, Wallace. *Furniture of the Pilgrim Century.* New York: Dover Publications, Inc., 1965.

Peterka, John and Lillian. *Ideas for the Experienced Caner.* Swisher, IA: Self-published, 1975. Pamphlet.

—. *Ideas for the Experienced Caner, #2.* Cedar Rapids, IA: Self-published, 1977. Pamphlet.

Shea, John G. *The American Shakers and Their Furniture.* New York: Van Nostrand Reinhold Co., 1971.

Sober, Marion Burr. *Chair Weaving.* Plymouth, MI: Self-published, 1964. Pamphlet.

Thonet Bentwood & Other Furniture. New York: Dover Publications, Inc., 1980. Catalog.

Wright, Florence E. *Three Centuries of Furniture.* Cornell Extension Bulletin 672. Ithaca, NY: Cornell University, 1950. Pamphlet.